We don't think you're
a clueless person but a
baker — maybe ☺
Merry Christmas
2017
Diane +
Terry

The Clueless Baker

The Clueless Baker

Learning to Bake from Scratch
Revised and Updated

EVELYN RAAB

FIREFLY BOOKS

A FIREFLY BOOK

Published by Firefly Books Ltd. 2013

First printing

Publisher Cataloging-in-Publication Data (U.S.)

Raab, Evelyn.
The clueless baker : learning to bake from scratch / Evelyn Raab.
Rev. ed.
[216] p. : ill. ; cm.
Includes index.
Summary: Topics include the fundamentals of baking, baking substitutions, troubleshooting, and recipes for breads, muffins, biscuits, cookies, pastries, cakes and pies.
ISBN-13: 978-1-77085-245-7 (pbk.)
1. Baking. 2. Breads. 3. Desserts. I. Title.
641.815 dc22   TX765.R333 2013

Library and Archives Canada Cataloguing in Publication

Raab, Evelyn
The clueless baker : learning to bake from scratch / Evelyn Raab. -- Rev. ed.
Includes index.
ISBN 978-1-77085-245-7
1. Baking. I. Title.
TX763.R318 2013   641.81'5   C2013-901246-X

Published in the United States by
Firefly Books (U.S.) Inc.
P.O. Box 1338, Ellicott Station
Buffalo, New York 14205

Published in Canada by
Firefly Books Ltd.
50 Staples Avenue, Unit 1
Richmond Hill, Ontario L4B 0A7

Illustrations: Clive Dobson and George A. Walker (pages 44, 95, 104, 205)
Cover design: Hartley Millson

Printed in Canada

The publisher gratefully acknowledges the financial support for our publishing program by the Government of Canada through the Canada Book Fund as administered by the Department of Canadian Heritage.

To my husband George, an enthusiastic (but brutally honest) guinea pig, who wouldn't let me bake anything with cloves in it; and to my two intrepid sons, Dustin and Jared, who bravely struggled to try and keep up with the sheer volume of cookies that were produced during the writing of this book.

Contents

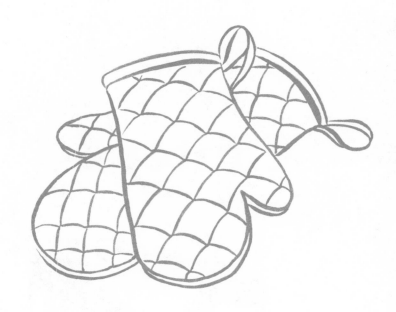

Getting Started

The oven looms before you. A darkened abyss. *The gates of hell*. You know — *you just know* — that whatever you put in there is doomed. Doomed and ruined. It will burn. Or collapse. Probably both.

Plus, your house will burn down. Which is just as well, because after the mess you made of the kitchen it would take ten lifetimes to clean it up, anyway. There is flour on the floor. Batter on the walls. Broken eggs in the sink (it was an accident). You're missing a spatula (you pray it didn't get baked into the cake). The phone is ringing, but you can't find it.

Okay. Take a deep breath and relax. Help has arrived.

What you need are some decent recipes, a good attitude and a plan. Baking can be — *should be* — fun. Also easy. It should be neither traumatic nor terrifying. And at the end of it, you should have something delicious to eat. Which is, after all, the point of the whole thing.

Let's begin with the plan.

Baking — The Eleven-Step Program

1. *First, decide what you want to make.* This is the easy part. Do you feel like brownies, or are you having a focaccia kind of day? Do you want to throw something together really fast, or do you feel like taking your time and wallowing in the experience? Make up your mind, would you, please?

2. *Choose a recipe.* This book is full of them.

3. *Read through the recipe.* Do you have all the ingredients you'll need? Are you sure? Do you have the right size baking pan? Will you need an electric mixer? Blender? Baking parchment? Does the dough have to chill before baking? Rise? Meditate? How long does it have to bake? Will whatever-it-is be ready to eat right away, or will you have to let it cool? It's all there in the recipe — just take the time to read it.

4. *Preheat the oven.* Now. Before you do anything else. Go.

5. *Assemble the ingredients.* Take every single ingredient out and arrange it in a tasteful and attractive manner on your kitchen counter. If you are an obsessive type, you might even measure the ingredients into individual bowls and set them out in the order you'll use them. But let's not get ahead of ourselves here.

6. *Prepare your baking pan.* Grease it, flour it, line it with parchment paper if the recipe calls for it. Have some bowls ready; get out your mixer (find the beater thingies!); grab the measuring cups and a spoon. You don't want to be groping around your junk drawer for a spatula when you're up to your elbows in batter.

7. *Okay, now you can start.* Begin at the beginning and follow the instructions *exactly*. This is no time to be creative. At least, not the first time. If you decide to bake the same thing again, you can be more adventurous — substitute ingredients, take liberties and go rogue. But follow the directions at least once — you may even learn something.

8. *Keep your eye on the oven.* Set a timer and make sure you can hear it ring from wherever you'll be. If necessary, buy yourself a dollar-store timer that you can take with you out to the yard or down to the basement. You *think* you'll remember to take the

muffins out of the oven, but honestly, you won't. Not until you smell smoke. At which point it will be, alas, too late.

9. *Do the toothpick test; tap the top of the loaf; stick a knife in the pie*. Do whatever the recipe tells you, to make sure your whatchamacallit is baked to perfection.

10. *Ta-da! Done.* Remove your delicious baked item(s) from the oven, carefully remove from the baking pan(s) and let cool on a rack for as long as you can stand.

11. *Enjoy*. You earned it.

Bare Necessities, Electric Gizmos and Extra Added Widgets

Baking equipment tends to be pretty simple. You've got your pans, your bowls, your spatulas. Most of the things you need are inexpensive and easy to find. If you're on a really tight budget, you can shop at secondhand stores and garage sales. If you recently inherited a fortune, you can blow it all at a fancy kitchenware store. Either way, your muffins will turn out just fine.

Bare Necessities
✓ two 8 or 9-inch (20 or 23 cm) round cake pans
✓ one 9 x 13-inch (23 x 33 cm) rectangular baking pan
✓ one 8 or 9-inch (20 or 23 cm) square baking pan
✓ two 9 x 5-inch (23 x 13 cm) loaf pans
✓ two 10 x 15 inch (25 x 38 cm) cookie sheets with 1-inch (2 cm) sides
✓ one muffin pan with 12 cups (or two with 6 cups each)
✓ one 8-cup (2 liter) bundt or tube pan (approximately 9 inches/23 cm diameter)
✓ one 9 or 10-inch (23 or 25 cm) springform pan with removable sides
✓ one or two wire grid cooling racks
✓ one set of Official Measuring Spoons (imperial or metric or both)
✓ one set of individual steel or plastic measuring cups (in graduated sizes: ¼ cup, ⅓ cup, ½ cup and 1 cup, or metric equivalents)
✓ heatproof glass measuring cups (1 cup/250 ml and 4 cups/1 liter)
✓ mixing bowls — stainless steel or glass — at least 2 really big ones (4 quarts/4 liters) and as many smaller ones as you have room for

- ✓ a bunch of small glass or plastic bowls for organizing ingredients
- ✓ whisk
- ✓ rubber bowl scrapers (spatulas)
- ✓ wooden spoons
- ✓ flour sifter
- ✓ pastry blender (that chopper thingy for making pastry dough)
- ✓ pastry brush
- ✓ wooden rolling pin
- ✓ cookie cutters
- ✓ baking parchment paper

Electric Gizmos
- ✓ electric mixer — either handheld or countertop model
- ✓ blender — traditional or stick type
- ✓ food processor

Extra Added Widgets (for the seriously motivated baker)
- ✓ pastry bag and decorating tips
- ✓ one 10-inch (25 cm) tart pan with removable sides
- ✓ one 10-inch (25 cm) two-part tube pan (angel cake pan) with removable sides
- ✓ electronic digital scale (to weigh ingredients)

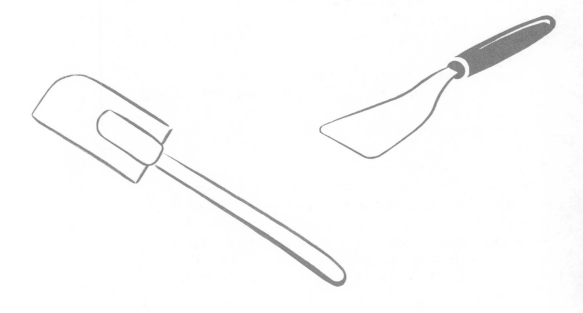

The food processor: is it good for anything besides shredding cheese?

Yes, use your food processor to:

Cut shortening into dry ingredients when you're making pastry or biscuits

Combine butter, sugar and flour to make crumble toppings

Cream together butter, sugar and eggs for cookies or cakes

Mix and knead yeast bread dough

Chop nuts

Slice apples or other fruit for pies

Shred carrots or apples for cake or muffins

Uh, yeah, shred cheese

Roughly chop chocolate

Puree bananas for cakes or muffins

Make graham cracker or other cookie crumbs

No, don't try to use your food processor to:

Whip cream

Beat egg whites

Grate lemon or orange peel

Beat cake batter

Make a piña colada

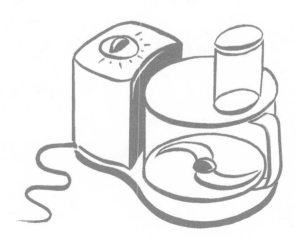

The Essential Clueless Baking Cupboard

It's three in the morning. It suddenly occurs to you that you can't possibly get through the night without chocolate chip cookies. Homemade ones. Warm. Right now. Aren't you glad you keep ingredients in the house?

Absolute necessities

- ✓ all-purpose white flour (regular or unbleached)
- ✓ all-purpose whole wheat flour
- ✓ granulated white sugar
- ✓ brown sugar (golden or dark brown)
- ✓ icing (confectioners') sugar
- ✓ baking powder
- ✓ baking soda
- ✓ quick-rise instant dry yeast granules
- ✓ butter
- ✓ vegetable oil
- ✓ solid vegetable shortening (preferably trans-fat free)
- ✓ eggs
- ✓ milk
- ✓ semisweet chocolate chips
- ✓ semisweet baking chocolate
- ✓ unsweetened baking chocolate
- ✓ unsweetened cocoa powder
- ✓ quick-cooking rolled oats (not instant)
- ✓ pure vanilla extract
- ✓ peanut butter
- ✓ cinnamon
- ✓ raisins
- ✓ walnuts
- ✓ nonstick baking spray

Noncompulsory ingredients

- ✓ cake and pastry flour
- ✓ cornmeal
- ✓ cornstarch
- ✓ graham cracker crumbs
- ✓ chocolate wafer crumbs
- ✓ natural bran
- ✓ honey
- ✓ corn syrup
- ✓ molasses
- ✓ whipping cream
- ✓ sour cream
- ✓ buttermilk
- ✓ yogurt
- ✓ cream cheese
- ✓ cream of tartar
- ✓ ginger
- ✓ nutmeg
- ✓ pecans
- ✓ almonds
- ✓ hazelnuts
- ✓ dried cranberries
- ✓ dates
- ✓ coconut
- ✓ lemons

Specialty ingredients

- ✓ white chocolate chips or chunks
- ✓ poppy seeds
- ✓ sesame seeds
- ✓ instant coffee powder
- ✓ phyllo pastry
- ✓ gluten-free flour mixture
- ✓ brown or white rice flour

Emergency substitutions

Can it be true? You're out of chocolate? Baking powder? Brown sugar? Don't panic — help is on the way. Not every ingredient is replaceable, but the following substitutions will allow you to continue baking despite the missing whatever-it-is. In some cases, the finished product will be almost identical. Some substitutions can produce a slightly different flavor or texture in the finished product. Maybe a better one — you never know.

1 oz. (28 g) unsweetened chocolate
3 tbsp. (45 ml) unsweetened cocoa powder + 1 tbsp. (15 ml) vegetable oil or melted butter

1 oz. (28 g) semisweet chocolate
3 tbsp. (45 ml) unsweetened cocoa powder + 1 tbsp. (15 ml) vegetable oil or melted butter + 1 tbsp. (15 ml) sugar
1 oz. (28 g) unsweetened chocolate + 1 tbsp. (15 ml) sugar
2 tbsp. (30 ml) semisweet chocolate chips

1 cup (250 ml) semisweet chocolate chips
6 oz. (170 g) semisweet chocolate chunks or bar

1 whole egg
2 egg whites + 1 tsp. (5 ml) vegetable oil
2 egg yolks + 1 tbsp. (15 ml) water
¼ cup (60 ml) egg mixture (real egg or substitute)

1 cup (250 ml) vegetable oil
1 cup (250 ml) butter or margarine
1 cup (250 ml) solid vegetable shortening
1 cup (250 ml) lard

1 tsp. (5 ml) baking powder
½ tsp. (2 ml) cream of tartar + ¼ tsp. (1 ml) baking soda

1 cup (250 ml) buttermilk
1 cup (250 ml) plain yogurt
1 tbsp. (15 ml) lemon juice or vinegar + milk to equal 1 cup (250 ml)

1 cup (250 ml) sour cream
3 tbsp. (45 ml) butter + buttermilk or yogurt to equal 1 cup (250 ml)
1 cup (250 ml) Greek-style yogurt

1 cup (250 ml) brown sugar
1 cup (250 ml) granulated sugar + 2 tbsp. (30 ml) molasses
1 cup (250 ml) granulated sugar (with no molasses, flavor will be different)

1 cup (250 ml) corn syrup
1 cup (250 ml) granulated sugar + ¼ cup (60 ml) water
1 cup (250 ml) honey
1 cup (250 ml) maple syrup

1 cup (250 ml) molasses
1 cup (250 ml) honey or corn syrup (flavor will be different)

1 cup (250 ml) cake and pastry flour
1 cup (250 ml) minus 2 tbsp. (30 ml) all-purpose flour

1 tsp. (5 ml) allspice
Equal parts cinnamon, nutmeg and cloves to total 1 tsp. (5 ml)

The Basics About Some Basics

What kind of sugar, exactly? How big an egg? How much salt? Here are a few additional details you may need to know before you begin baking.

Eggs
Whenever eggs appear in a recipe, we mean standard large eggs. White or brown or blue — shell color doesn't affect the taste, so just choose whatever best matches your décor. Freshness counts — a fresh egg will separate more easily, and beat up fluffier.

If small or medium eggs are on sale, you can use them instead of large eggs: one large egg measures about ¼ cup (60 ml). Crack your small or medium eggs into a measuring cup so you can tell how many eggs you'll need to use in your recipe. For a recipe that calls for 2 eggs, you'll need to use a total of ½ cup (125 ml) liquid egg.

Butter
We love butter. Because it tastes wonderful. Because it bakes beautifully. And because it's a natural product. Unsalted butter is preferred for baking since it allows you to control the amount of salt in the finished product. If, for any reason, you wish to avoid butter, you can substitute margarine for butter in most recipes. The results will be similar, but the flavor may be slightly different.

Margarine

Look for margarine that is trans-fat free and buy the best quality that you can afford. If you prefer to avoid dairy ingredients, be sure to read the label carefully: milk ingredients in food products may be hidden in the ingredient list — look for lactase, casein, whey and milk solids, which are all secret code words for milk. If you see the word *pareve* on the label, you can be sure the product contains no milk or other animal ingredients.

Sugar

When a recipe calls for granulated sugar, that means ordinary white sugar. Comes in bags or cartons. The usual stuff. If a recipe requires brown sugar, you can use either light or dark brown sugar. Dark brown contains more molasses and has a stronger flavor; light brown (or golden brown) is milder but still flavorful — use whichever one you like. You may occasionally come across a recipe that calls for *caster sugar*. This is a finely granulated sugar often used in British recipes. You can substitute "instant dissolving" or "fruit sugar" for caster sugar, or just use regular granulated sugar — it'll work out fine either way.

Salt

Oddly enough, a pinch of salt can bring out the sweetness in a sweet recipe. Other than that, it has no scientific purpose when you're baking cookies or cakes, so add it if you want or leave it out. In savory (nonsweet) recipes — bread or focaccia, for example — salt really does enhance the flavor, and I recommend that you use it when called for in the ingredient list, although you can adjust the amount of salt to suit your taste.

Whipping cream or heavy cream

We're talking cream with a butterfat content of about 35 percent. The luscious stuff that whips into fluffy clouds of deliciousness. If you're not planning to whip the cream, however, you can usually substitute a lower fat cream (10, 15 or 18 percent), if you prefer.

Flour

Is nothing ever simple? You'll definitely need flour. But what kind of flour? Or didn't you know you had a choice?

For general baking purposes, we mean wheat flour. It's made from (surprise!) wheat and is available in many different types. Each type is best suited for a specific purpose.

Here is a list of the most commonly used types of wheat flour:

All-purpose white flour is the most widely available kind of flour. It comes in small bags or in bulk and is sold under many different brand names. If the bag says nothing else (such as unbleached or whole wheat), you can assume you've got all-purpose white flour. This product has been milled; the bran has been sifted out; and the flour has been bleached by chemical means to make it dazzlingly white. Vitamins and whatnot are added to replace some of the nutrients that were lost in the refining process. As the name suggests, all-purpose white flour is suitable for most baking purposes unless the recipe specifies another type of flour.

All-purpose unbleached white flour is white flour that hasn't been subjected to a bleaching process and therefore remains creamy white in color. All-purpose unbleached white flour can be used in any recipe that calls for all-purpose flour. Some people prefer to use it because it has undergone less processing than bleached flour.

Cake and pastry flour is made from soft wheat — a variety of wheat that has a lower gluten (see below) and protein content. It's often recommended for baking cakes and pastry, where you're more interested in lightness and fluffiness than in sturdiness. With only one exception, regular all-purpose flour is perfectly adequate for every recipe in this book. The one exception is Angel Food Cake, which is just delicate enough to require cake and pastry flour.

Whole wheat flour is milled kernels of hulled whole wheat. Period. Nothing has been taken out. The outside layer of bran and the wheat germ are both left in the flour. Whole wheat flour is darker in color than white flour, and has a hearty wheat flavor and a coarser texture. It contains all the nutrients found in wheat and provides a hefty dose of fiber. Use whole wheat flour by itself or mixed with white flour when baking breads or cookies — you may want to experiment with different combinations until you find a mixture that you like. Whole wheat flour should be stored in the refrigerator or freezer to prevent it from developing an off taste — the oil in the wheat germ can turn funny after a while at warm room temperature.

Gluten-free all-purpose flour is a wheat-free product that can be substituted for regular wheat-based all-purpose flour in many recipes. Gluten-free flour is usually some blend of garbanzo flour, potato starch, tapioca starch, sorghum flour, rice flour and/or cornstarch, among other things. Different commercial brands of gluten-free flour are made of different combinations of ingredients. As a very general rule, if a recipe contains ½ cup (125 ml) or less of regular flour, you can substitute the same quantity of gluten-free flour. The results will probably be slightly different from the original version of the recipe, but if you must avoid gluten, it's definitely worth experimenting.

Chocolate. Need we say more?

Well, yes, actually. We need to say lots more. Because there's lots to say.

Chocolate is made from the fruit of a tropical bush. You pick the beans, whack off their shells, roast them and then squeeze out the juice — from which, eventually, chocolate is made. The juice, technically called *cocoa liquor*, contains both the cocoa solids (the chocolate-flavored part) and cocoa butter (the creamy smooth melt-in-your-mouth part). These two substances are combined in different proportions, with varying amounts of sugar, to make your basic hunk of chocolate.

Unsweetened chocolate is a mixture of cocoa solids and cocoa butter. No sugar. It has an intense chocolate flavor and is often used in baking when you're looking for a big chocolate hit without added sweetness. It comes in 1-ounce (28 g) squares (usually in a package of six or eight, which you can find in the baking aisle of the supermarket), or in chunks or squares in a bulk food store. It is absolutely *not* delicious until you do something with it — a fact that anyone who has accidentally taken a bite of unsweetened chocolate can confirm.

Semisweet (or bittersweet) chocolate is a mixture of cocoa solids, cocoa butter and sugar (along with various other ingredients added for flavor and texture). Semisweet chocolate contains more sugar than bittersweet chocolate does, but they're both deliciously edible and are interchangeable in recipes. Semisweet chocolate is commonly sold in packages of eight 1-ounce (28 g) squares, or in the form of large and small bars meant for eating. It's often better to buy a big bar of good-quality eating chocolate than a package of baking chocolate squares, but you'll need an accurate kitchen scale to weigh the right amount for your recipe.

Chocolate chips are usually semisweet chocolate specially formulated to hold its shape when baked in a cookie or cake. In general, you can usually substitute semisweet chocolate chips for an equal weight (hello, digital scale!) of semisweet baking chocolate chunks or bars in recipes where you melt the chocolate. See page 15 for equivalent amounts when using chocolate chips in place of semisweet baking chocolate (and vice versa).

Milk chocolate is mild, creamy and very sweet. It's made with more sugar than semisweet chocolate is and contains milk solids, as well as other ingredients for flavor and texture. Only occasionally used in baking, milk chocolate is usually just munched in the form of chocolate bars and Easter bunnies. Even though it doesn't pack a huge chocolate wallop, you still gotta love it, because, after all, it *is* chocolate.

White chocolate is pure cocoa butter mixed with sugar and a few other odds and ends for flavor and texture. The cocoa solids (the brown part that tastes like chocolate) have been left out of the picture. A good-quality white chocolate tastes rich and creamy, and is available in chips, chunks, disks and bars. White chocolate can't be used as a substitute for other types of chocolate — it's a different animal altogether.

Unsweetened cocoa powder is basically just processed cocoa solids that have been ground up to a powder. No sugar, no cocoa butter, no nothing else. It is often used in baking to add a serious chocolate punch with no additional fat or sweetness. Very handy. It's also easy to use, since it can often be mixed with the dry ingredients in a recipe. Unsweetened cocoa powder can be substituted for unsweetened baking chocolate, but you'll have to add some fat (oil, butter or shortening) to take the place of the missing cocoa butter (see page 15).

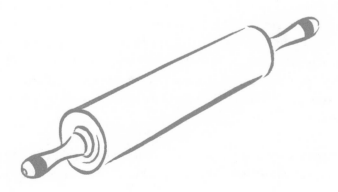

Quick Breads and Yeast Breads

Is there anything more straightforward, more honest, than a loaf of bread? Real bread. Made with actual flour, mixed personally and kneaded with your own hands. Woven into a braid or squashed into a loaf pan, sprinkled with seeds or glazed with egg yolk, served warm. With butter. Go ahead — have a slice. You know you can't resist.

Quick Breads

Beer Bread

You couldn't bring yourself to throw it out, could you? That open bottle of beer that's been at the back of the fridge for two weeks. Now you don't have to. This delicious bread is best served warm.

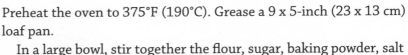

3 cups	(750 ml)	all-purpose flour
3 tbsp.	(45 ml)	granulated sugar
1 tbsp.	(15 ml)	baking powder
1 tsp.	(5 ml)	salt
½ tsp.	(2 ml)	baking soda
1 bottle		(12 oz./341 ml) beer, flat is fine (fizzy is fine too)

Optional ingredients: poppy seeds, sesame seeds, caraway seeds, chopped sundried tomatoes, chopped olives, crumbled herbs

Preheat the oven to 375°F (190°C). Grease a 9 x 5-inch (23 x 13 cm) loaf pan.

In a large bowl, stir together the flour, sugar, baking powder, salt and baking soda. Add the beer and any optional ingredients you like, and stir until thoroughly mixed into a gluey batter. Dump batter into the prepared loaf pan and bake for 45 to 50 minutes, until golden brown on top and no longer gooey in the center (do the toothpick test — page 23).

Remove loaf from pan and serve warm, or let cool on a rack and serve later. Whatever.

Makes 1 unbelievably easy loaf of bread.

Whole Wheat Positive
You can substitute whole wheat flour for all or part of the all-purpose flour in this recipe. Start with a small proportion, and if you like the result, you can use more whole wheat flour next time.

Great Pumpkin Bread

Make this loaf with canned pumpkin (the kind you use for pies) or with your own homemade pumpkin puree (see page 189). You can even use leftover mashed butternut or other baked winter squash if you happen to have some hanging around the fridge.

1½ cups	(375 ml)	granulated sugar
½ cup	(125 ml)	vegetable oil
2		eggs
1 cup	(250 ml)	pumpkin puree (canned or homemade)
1½ cups	(375 ml)	all-purpose flour
½ tsp.	(2 ml)	cinnamon
½ tsp.	(2 ml)	nutmeg
½ tsp.	(2 ml)	baking soda
½ tsp.	(2 ml)	baking powder
½ cup	(125 ml)	chopped walnuts or shelled pumpkin seeds (optional)

Preheat the oven to 350°F (180°C). Grease a 9 x 5-inch (23 x 13 cm) loaf pan.

Combine the sugar, oil and eggs in a large mixing bowl. Beat with an electric mixer until well blended, about 2 or 3 minutes. Add the pumpkin puree and beat for another minute or two.

In another bowl, stir together the flour, cinnamon, nutmeg, baking soda and baking powder. Add this to the pumpkin mixture, in 2 or 3 additions, beating after each addition. Stir in the walnuts or pumpkin seeds if you're using them.

Spoon the batter into the prepared loaf pan and bake for about 60 to 70 minutes, or until a toothpick stuck into the middle of the loaf comes out clean. Let cool in the baking pan for about 10 minutes, then remove from pan and cool completely on a wire rack.

Makes 1 heartwarming 9 x 5-inch (23 x 13 cm) loaf.

Whole Wheat Positive
You can substitute whole wheat flour for all or part of the all-purpose flour in this recipe. Start with a small proportion, and if you like the result, you can use more whole wheat flour next time.

The Famous Toothpick Test

Relax, you don't have to study for this. The toothpick test is a simple way of finding out whether the cake you're baking is ready to come out of the oven. Here's what you do.

Open the oven door, and without removing the pan from the rack, take a clean toothpick and stick it into the cake, bread or muffin, as close to the middle as possible. If what you're baking is done, the toothpick will be come out clean, with no batter clinging to it. If the toothpick is coated with batter, the cake (or whatever it is) needs to bake a bit longer. Slide the pan back into the oven and give it another five minutes, then test again. Repeat until your whatchamacallit passes the test.

Ridiculously Easy Cheese Bread

Variation

Add chopped jalapeño peppers, onions, olives or sundried tomatoes to the batter when you add the cheese. Or stir some coarsely ground black pepper, crushed red pepper flakes, oregano or rosemary into the flour mixture.

A bowl of homemade soup, a green salad. A loaf of this bread. There. Dinner.

2 cups	(500 ml)	all-purpose flour
4 tsp.	(20 ml)	baking powder
1 tbsp.	(15 ml)	granulated sugar
½ tsp.	(2 ml)	salt
1¼ cups	(300 ml)	shredded cheese (sharp cheddar, Monterey Jack, Swiss — actually any natural cheese)
1 cup	(250 ml)	milk
1		egg
2 tbsp.	(30 ml)	vegetable oil
1 tsp.	(5 ml)	Dijon mustard

Preheat the oven to 375°F (190°C). Grease a 9 x 5-inch (23 x 13 cm) loaf pan.

In a large bowl, stir together the flour, baking powder, sugar and salt until combined. Dump in the shredded cheese and toss to mix.

In another bowl, whisk together the milk, egg, vegetable oil and mustard. All at once, pour the egg mixture into the flour mixture and stir just until all the ingredients are moistened. The batter will be lumpy — but that's okay.

Spoon batter into the prepared loaf pan and bake for 35 to 40 minutes, or until the top is lightly browned. Allow bread to cool for about 10 minutes before attempting to remove from the pan.

Makes 1 ridiculously easy but totally cheesy loaf.

Whole Wheat Positive
You can substitute whole wheat flour for all or part of the all-purpose flour in this recipe. Start with a small proportion, and if you like the result, you can use more whole wheat flour next time.

Irish Soda Bread with Cranberries

This bread is at its best when served warm, straight from the oven, with plenty of butter. And in the (highly unlikely) event that there's any left over, it makes great breakfast toast the next day.

3¾ cups	(900 ml)	all-purpose flour (plus additional for kneading)
¼ cup	(60 ml)	brown sugar
1½ tbsp.	(22 ml)	baking powder
½ tsp.	(2 ml)	baking soda
1 tsp.	(5 ml)	salt
¾ cup	(175 ml)	dried cranberries, chopped (or raisins or dried currants)
2 cups	(500 ml)	buttermilk
1		egg

Preheat the oven to 375°F (190°C). Grease a cookie sheet or line it with parchment paper.

In a large bowl, mix the flour, brown sugar, baking powder, baking soda and salt. Add the dried cranberries and mix well.

In another bowl, whisk together the buttermilk and the egg. Pour the buttermilk mixture into the flour mixture and stir until everything is well blended. At this point, the dough will be pretty soft — that's okay. Sprinkle some additional flour onto the counter or table (or wherever you like to work) and dump the dough onto this floured surface. Sprinkle the dough with a bit of flour and lightly knead it about 10 times — just enough to make the dough smooth-ish and pliable. Gently shape it into a round loaf and place it on the prepared cookie sheet. With a very sharp knife, cut a shallow X into the top of the loaf. This will allow the loaf to expand in a tasteful and decorative manner as it bakes rather than splitting weirdly.

Bake for 50 to 55 minutes, or until the loaf is nicely browned and a toothpick poked into the middle of it comes out clean. Let cool for a few minutes before devouring.

Makes 1 large round loaf.

Whole Wheat Positive

You can substitute whole wheat flour for all or part of the all-purpose flour in this recipe. Start with a small proportion, and if you like the result, you can use more whole wheat flour next time.

Don't Cry Over Sour Milk

Recipes will occasionally require sour milk as an ingredient. But not the kind of sour milk that happens when you leave a quart on the coffee table for three days. That's spoiled milk and you should throw it away. Sour milk is something else altogether.

In baking, sour milk, buttermilk or yogurt provides the acidity that your baking soda needs to act as a leavening agent — the stuff that makes your quick breads and muffins rise. As a rule, you can use the three interchangeably in most recipes (although yogurt should be thinned with a small amount of milk to make it pourable).

But what if you don't have any of those ingredients? Well, you can make your own sour milk. Here's how: Measure 1 tbsp. (15 ml) of vinegar into a 1 cup (250 ml) measuring cup, then add enough milk to fill the cup. Stir, then let sit for about 5 minutes. It will curdle and look disgusting. Congratulations, you are now the proud owner of some sour milk, which you can use in any recipe that calls for sour milk or buttermilk.

Unpretentious Zucchini Bread

It's not easy being green. The gentle zucchini, too often the butt of callous jokes, doesn't deserve such mockery. How can we help this humble vegetable develop a true sense of self-worth in this cruel world? Turn it into a simple but delicious bread — that's how.

2 cups	(500 ml)	all-purpose flour
¾ cup	(175 ml)	brown sugar
2 tsp.	(10 ml)	baking powder
½ tsp.	(2 ml)	baking soda
½ cup	(125 ml)	vegetable oil
¼ cup	(60 ml)	milk
1		egg
1½ cups	(375 ml)	coarsely grated zucchini (about 2 small-ish ones)
½ cup	(125 ml)	chopped walnuts
1 tsp.	(5 ml)	grated lime or lemon zest

Preheat the oven to 350°F (180°C). Grease a 9 x 5-inch (23 x 13 cm) loaf pan.

In a large bowl, mix the flour, brown sugar, baking powder and baking soda.

In another bowl, whisk together the vegetable oil, milk and egg.

Add the egg mixture to the flour mixture and stir just until the ingredients are moistened. Now stir in the zucchini, walnuts and lime or lemon zest, and mix until everything is evenly distributed in the batter. (This is a very thick batter — but that's okay. The grated zucchini will release moisture as it bakes.)

Dump into the prepared loaf pan and bake for 55 to 60 minutes, or until the top is golden brown and it passes the toothpick test (see page 23).

Remove loaf from the baking pan and let cool completely before slicing. If you can possibly resist eating it immediately, it actually improves wrapped in foil and left to sit overnight.

Makes one 9 x 5-inch (23 x 13 cm) unpretentious loaf.

Whole Wheat Positive
You can substitute whole wheat flour for all or part of the all-purpose flour in this recipe. Start with a small proportion, and if you like the result, you can use more whole wheat flour next time.

Blender Banana Bread

Extra extra!

Want to throw in some chopped nuts? Chocolate chips? Raisins? Go ahead! It'll be just fine. Add about ¾ cup (175 ml) of any one (or mixture) of the above to the batter when you combine the wet and dry ingredients. It's your banana bread now, baby.

Hey — look. There. Beside the microwave. Under the oranges. Isn't that a bunch of mushy old bananas? Yes! It's banana bread time.

1¼ cups	**(300 ml)**	**all-purpose flour**
1 cup	**(250 ml)**	**granulated sugar**
1 tsp.	**(5 ml)**	**baking powder**
½ tsp.	**(2 ml)**	**baking soda**
2		**seriously ripe bananas, peeled**
½ cup	**(125 ml)**	**vegetable oil**
2		**eggs**

Preheat the oven to 350°F (180°C). Grease a 9 x 5-inch (23 x 13 cm) loaf pan.

In a large bowl, stir together the flour, sugar, baking powder and baking soda.

Put the bananas, oil and eggs into the container of a blender and blend until smooth. Pour the blended banana mixture into the flour mixture and stir just until thoroughly combined.

Spoon the batter into the prepared loaf pan and bake for 55 to 65 minutes, until a toothpick poked into the middle of the loaf comes out clean. Remove from the pan and place on a rack to cool.

Makes 1 simply superb loaf of banana bread.

Whole Wheat Positive
You can substitute whole wheat flour for all or part of the all-purpose flour in this recipe. Start with a small proportion, and if you like the result, you can use more whole wheat flour next time.

Cranberry Orange Bread

A lovely thing to serve thinly sliced at your next tea party. Not planning a tea party? Pity.

2 cups	(500 ml)	all-purpose flour
1 cup	(250 ml)	granulated sugar
1½ tsp.	(7 ml)	baking powder
½ tsp.	(2 ml)	baking soda
1		medium orange (juice squeezed and zest grated)
1		egg
¼ cup	(60 ml)	vegetable oil
1 cup	(250 ml)	fresh or frozen cranberries, cut into halves
½ cup	(125 ml)	chopped walnuts

Preheat the oven to 350°F (180°C). Grease a 9 x 5-inch (23 x 13 cm) loaf pan.

In a large bowl, stir together the flour, sugar, baking powder and baking soda.

Grate the zest from the orange and set it aside. Squeeze the orange juice into a measuring cup and add just enough water to measure ¾ cup (175 ml) of liquid. Pour this into a small bowl, and add the grated orange zest, egg and vegetable oil. Whisk until well blended.

Add the juice mixture to the flour mixture and stir just until everything is moistened. Stir in the cranberries and walnuts — mix just until combined. Scoop batter into the prepared loaf pan and bake for 55 to 60 minutes, or until the loaf is golden brown on top and passes the toothpick test (see page 23).

Remove loaf from the baking pan and let cool completely before slicing. In fact, this tastes even better if you wrap it in foil and let it sit overnight. No really.

Makes one 9 x 5 inch (23 x 13 cm) loaf.

Whole Wheat Positive
You can substitute whole wheat flour for all or part of the all-purpose flour in this recipe. Start with a small proportion, and if you like the result, you can use more whole wheat flour next time.

Painless Nut Chopping

Painless for you, that is.

Measure your walnuts, pecans, almonds or hazelnuts into a zip-top plastic bag. Roll with a rolling pin until the nuts are chopped the way you want them. *Ta-da!*

Blueberry Lemon Bread

Grate first, squeeze later

Whenever a recipe calls for both the grated zest and the juice of a lemon, lime or orange, always grate first, then squeeze afterward. You can easily squeeze a lemon after it's been zested, but you just can't zest a squoozen one.

You've invited Great-Aunt Gertrude to lunch. What on earth are you going to serve? Well, tuna casserole, of course. And with her tea, this lemony bread. She'll be so impressed.

1		lemon (zest grated, juice squeezed)
1¼ cups	(300 ml)	granulated sugar, divided
1½ cups	(375 ml)	all-purpose flour
2 tsp.	(10 ml)	baking powder
¼ cup	(60 ml)	butter, softened
2		eggs
½ cup	(125 ml)	milk
1 cup	(250 ml)	blueberries, fresh or frozen (if frozen, don't thaw)

Too much of a good thing?

Even if you only need a small amount of lemon juice for your recipe, you may as well go right ahead and squeeze the whole thing. Freeze the extra juice in an ice cube tray and store the cubes in a plastic bag in the freezer to use another time.

Preheat the oven to 350°F (180°C). Grease a 9 x 5-inch (23 x 13 cm) loaf pan.

Grate the zest from the lemon into a small bowl and set aside. Squeeze the juice into a microwave-safe glass measuring cup or bowl. Add ¼ cup (60 ml) of the sugar to the lemon juice. Set aside.

In a bowl, stir together the flour and the baking powder.

In a large mixing bowl, combine the remaining 1 cup (250 ml) of sugar with the softened butter and beat with an electric mixer for 1 or 2 minutes, until fluffy. Add the eggs, 1 at a time, beating well after each. Add the grated lemon zest. Now add the flour mixture in 2 or 3 additions, alternating with the milk, beating until the batter is smooth. Quickly fold in the blueberries, mixing just until they're evenly distributed.

Pour batter into the prepared loaf pan and bake for 65 to 70 minutes, until the top is golden brown and a toothpick poked into the middle comes out clean. Don't remove the loaf from the pan yet!

Remember that little bowl with the lemon juice and sugar? Place it in the microwave and nuke on high power for 1 minute, stirring once or twice, until the sugar has dissolved and the mixture becomes syrupy. With a toothpick, poke holes all over the top of the baked loaf and gradually spoon the syrup over, allowing it to soak in. Let cool in the pan for about 30 minutes before removing to a rack to cool completely.

Makes 1 refreshingly lemony 9 x 5-inch (23 x 13 cm) loaf.

Whole Wheat Positive

You can substitute whole wheat flour for all or part of the all-purpose flour in this recipe. Start with a small proportion, and if you like the result, you can use more whole wheat flour next time.

Grease is not a four-letter word

It's happened to all of us. The cookies that stick to the cookie sheet. The cake (or worse — half of a cake) that refuses to exit the baking pan. The otherwise perfect loaf of bread that stubbornly resists all attempts to pry it loose from the mold.

It's your fault. If you had greased the pan properly, everything would have been fine.

For most baking, the fastest and easiest way to grease a pan is to use commercial nonstick vegetable oil cooking spray. It's a perfectly innocent product made from a combination of vegetable oil, lecithin and environmentally acceptable propellents. And most recycling programs will accept this type of spray can.

If you prefer to avoid nonstick spray, use either vegetable oil or melted shortening to grease your baking pans. Make sure you generously coat the baking pan — into the corners, up the sides — leaving no spot ungreased.

Butter, despite all its other wonderful qualities, is not a good choice for pan greasing because it contains water and milk solids, which can cause your delicious baked thing to stick or burn. So save it for spreading on a warm slice of freshly baked bread, where it will be truly appreciated.

Date Nut Bread in a Can

Chopping Dates (or, for that matter, raisins or dried apricots or other dried fruit)

This is a thankless, sticky task. Here's a way to make it easier.

Toss the dates with a little of the flour from the recipe until well coated. Then, using a pair of scissors, snip them into pieces. The flour should keep the bits of fruit from sticking to the scissors.

If you borrowed the scissors from the family sewing kit, don't forget to wash them well before returning them. Oh — and don't forget to return them.

Whole Wheat Positive
You can substitute whole wheat flour for all or part of the all-purpose flour in this recipe. Start with a small proportion, and if you like the result, you can use more whole wheat flour next time.

Delicious and adorable. Of course you can bake these breads in two regular loaf pans instead, if you don't want to mess around with cans — but the breads won't be nearly as cute.

1½ cups	(375 ml)	chopped, pitted dates
1 tsp.	(5 ml)	baking soda
1 cup	(250 ml)	boiling water
1 cup	(250 ml)	granulated sugar
1		egg
2 cups	(500 ml)	all-purpose flour
1 tsp.	(5 ml)	baking powder
1 tsp.	(5 ml)	vanilla extract
½ cup	(125 ml)	chopped walnuts
4		empty cans — soup or bean size (10 to 15 oz./300 to 425 ml, more or less)

Preheat the oven to 325°F (160°C).

Measure the chopped dates into a large mixing bowl and toss with the baking soda. Pour in the boiling water, stir well (it will foam a bit), then let the mixture sit until cool, about ½ hour.

Meanwhile, prepare your cans. Assuming that the top has already been removed, wash the cans out thoroughly (be really careful of the sharp edges). Grease the cans well. If you're not using cans, grease two 9 x 5-inch (23 x 13 cm) loaf pans.

When the date mixture is cool, add the sugar, egg, flour, baking powder and vanilla, and mix well. Stir in the chopped walnuts. Spoon the batter into the prepared cans or pans, dividing it equally among the cans (or pans). Place cans on a cookie sheet and bake for 30 to 35 minutes, or until a toothpick poked into the center of the bread comes out clean. If using loaf pans, just place on oven rack and increase baking time to 35 to 40 minutes, until done. Remove from the cans or pans and let cool completely on a rack. If you have trouble getting the breads out of the cans, remove the bottom of the can with a can opener and push the bread out from below.

Makes 4 nifty little round breads, perfect for tea party sandwiches (with cream cheese, please!) or to give as gifts.

Crummy Apple Bread

Make this crumble-topped loaf on a crisp fall afternoon. Not only does it taste delicious, but it will also make your house smell great while it's baking. Bonus.

2 cups	(500 ml)	all-purpose flour
2 tsp.	(10 ml)	baking powder
½ tsp.	(2 ml)	baking soda
1 cup	(250 ml)	granulated sugar
½ cup	(125 ml)	vegetable oil
2		eggs
2 tsp.	(10 ml)	vanilla extract
2 cups	(500 ml)	peeled, chopped apples (2 to 3 medium apples)
½ cup	(125 ml)	chopped walnuts
½ cup	(125 ml)	All-Purpose Crumble Topping (page 182)

Preheat the oven to 350°F (180°C). Grease a 9 x 5-inch (23 x 13 cm) loaf pan.

In a large mixing bowl, stir together the flour, baking powder and baking soda.

In a mixing bowl, whisk together the sugar, vegetable oil, eggs and vanilla until well blended and smooth. Add this to the flour mixture, stirring just until the dry ingredients are combined. Dump in the chopped apples and the walnuts, and stir just to mix.

Pour batter into the prepared loaf pan and sprinkle the top evenly with the crumble topping mixture. Bake for 60 to 70 minutes, until the crumble topping is golden brown and the loaf passes the toothpick test (page 23). Remove from the pan and let cool completely before attempting to slice it.

Makes 1 crummy 9 x 5-inch (23 x 13 cm) loaf.

Whole Wheat Positive
You can substitute whole wheat flour for all or part of the all-purpose flour in this recipe. Start with a small proportion, and if you like the result, you can use more whole wheat flour next time.

But what kind of apples?

There are so many different varieties of apple out there — in every color, size and shape. How on earth do you know what kind to use for your recipe?

Some people like McIntosh for pies; others like Cortland. Some like to use Rome for applesauce, Granny Smith for apple cake, Honeycrisp for eating fresh. With experience, you'll learn which type of apple you like to use for whatever you're making. In the meantime, whatever you have around will work out just fine. So go ahead — use whatever kind of apple is in the fruit bowl, and don't overthink it. (The only type of apple I don't recommend for baking is Red Delicious — save those for your lunch box.)

Yeast Breads

No-Knead Casserole Bread

Different is good

Because this bread hasn't been kneaded like a traditional loaf of bread, the texture will be somewhat different from what you might expect. A bit cakey — not quite as bready — but very delicious. Just thought you should know.

This bread requires no finicky kneading (is that the part that scares you?) and can easily be varied to suit your mood.

3½ cups	(875 ml)	all-purpose flour, divided
4½ tsp.	(22 ml)	(2 envelopes) quick-rise instant yeast
3 tbsp.	(45 ml)	granulated sugar
1 tsp.	(5 ml)	salt
1 cup	(250 ml)	milk
¾ cup	(175 ml)	water
¼ cup	(60 ml)	butter or vegetable oil
1		egg

In a large mixing bowl, stir together 2 cups (500 ml) of the flour (this is only part of the total amount of flour!) the dry yeast granules, sugar and salt.

In a saucepan, or in a microwave-safe bowl, combine the milk, water and butter or oil. Heat on the stove or in the microwave until very warm to the touch — don't boil. Add warm liquid to the flour mixture and beat with an electric mixer (or stir by hand with a wooden spoon) for a few minutes, until quite gooey. Add the egg and the remaining flour, and beat or stir until the mixture is extremely sticky and has become difficult to stir. Cover the bowl with plastic wrap and place it in a warm spot to rise until doubled in volume — 30 to 45 minutes. (See page 35 for suggestions on where to rise your yeast dough.)

With a wooden spoon, stir down the batter to deflate it. Dump into a well-greased 2-quart (2 liter) soufflé or casserole dish and let rise again, until not quite doubled in volume — 15 to 20 minutes.

Meanwhile, preheat the oven to 350°F (180°C).

Place the casserole dish in the oven and bake for 40 to 45 minutes, or until the bread is golden brown on top and sounds hollow when you tap the top with your finger. Let cool for a few minutes before removing from the baking dish.

Makes 1 large loaf.

Whole Wheat Positive
You can substitute whole wheat flour for all or part of the all-purpose flour in this recipe. Start with a small proportion, and if you like the result, you can use more whole wheat flour next time.

The Clueless Baker

Casserole Bread Variations

Raisin Casserole Bread

Stir 1 cup (250 ml) raisins into the batter just before the first rise.
Bake as for the basic bread.

Cheese Casserole Bread

Reduce the butter or oil to 2 tbsp. (30 ml). Add 1½ cups (375 ml)
grated sharp cheddar cheese to the batter when you beat in the egg.
Bake as for the basic bread.

Feta and Olive Casserole Bread

Substitute olive oil for the butter in the basic recipe. Stir 1 cup
(250 ml) pitted black olives (preferably kalamata or other brine-cured
ones) into the batter just before the first rise. Sprinkle the top of
the bread with ½ cup (125 ml) crumbled feta cheese just before the
second rise. Bake as for the basic bread.

Rosemary Parmesan Bread

Substitute olive oil for the butter in the basic recipe. Add ½ cup
(125 ml) grated Parmesan cheese and 1 tbsp. (15 ml) chopped fresh
rosemary to the batter before the first rise. Just before baking, brush
the top of the loaf with a bit of olive oil and sprinkle with coarse salt
and a bit more chopped rosemary. Bake as for the basic bread.

Getting a Rise Out of Your Dough

Fine. You've made the dough. Now where do you put it to rise? Here are some ideas:

✓ Fill a large pan or bowl with very hot tap water and place it in the bottom of your oven.
Do not turn the oven on. Place your dough in a bowl on a rack over the hot water. The
water will add both warmth and humidity to the oven and give your yeast dough a perfect environment in which to grow.

✓ Fill a measuring cup with water and place it in the microwave. Zap until it comes to a
boil, then shove it into a corner of the microwave. Put your bowl of dough into the microwave with the cup of water. Same deal — warmth and humidity.

✓ Cover your dough with plastic wrap (to keep the surface from drying out) and place the
bowl on top of your refrigerator (if there's room). The heat from the fridge motor can
often provide a lovely warm spot for dough to rise.

One Hundred Percent Whole Wheat Bread

Just Tell Me How Much Flour!

You probably won't notice it, but different flours contain different amounts of moisture. This may not be obvious when you're making cookies or cakes, but for some reason it makes a big difference when you're baking a yeast bread. One type of flour might absorb a lot more liquid than another type — causing the dough to be heavier and denser, or softer and stickier.

Most yeast bread recipes will tell you to add flour gradually, a bit at a time, until the dough reaches the right texture. And that's just what you should do. Begin with the smallest quantity of flour specified in the recipe and continue adding until the dough is smooth and elastic. You may not need the entire amount of flour listed in the recipe — or you may need more than it states.

Sorry. That's as specific as it gets. Bread baking is an art, not nuclear physics.

This whole wheat bread is neither overly dense nor aggressively healthy tasting. It's just delicious, hearty and spectacularly good for you.

8½ cups	(2 liters)	whole wheat flour (approximately), divided
4½ tsp.	(22 ml)	(2 envelopes) quick-rise instant yeast
2½ tsp.	(12 ml)	salt
1½ cups	(375 ml)	water
1½ cups	(375 ml)	milk
¼ cup	(60 ml)	honey, maple syrup or molasses
¼ cup	(60 ml)	butter or vegetable oil

In a large mixing bowl, stir together 4 cups (1 liter) of the flour (only part of the flour — pay attention!), the yeast and salt.

In a saucepan, or in a microwave-safe bowl, combine the water, milk honey (or other sweetener) and butter or oil. Heat on the stove or in the microwave until very warm to the touch — don't boil. Add warm liquid to the flour mixture and beat with an electric mixer for 2 minutes on high speed (or by hand with a wooden spoon) until it forms a gooey but homogenous dough. Now, stirring by hand with a wooden spoon, add the remaining flour, ½ cup (125 ml) at a time, until the dough becomes too difficult to stir. Turn the dough out onto a well-floured surface, and knead by hand until smooth and elastic, sprinkling with additional flour to keep the dough from sticking to either your hands or the table — about 6 to 8 minutes. When the dough feels just damp — not sticky — it's ready to rise. You might not need to use the entire amount of flour. (Properly kneaded dough should have about the same consistency as your earlobe when you pinch it.)

Place the dough in a large oiled bowl, and turn the dough over to oil the top. Cover with plastic wrap and place it in a warm spot to rise until doubled — about 30 to 45 minutes.

Now uncover the dough, make a fist and punch down to deflate it. Turn the dough out onto a floured surface and knead it a few times. Let rest while you prepare the baking pans.

Grease two 9 x 5-inch (23 x 13 cm) loaf pans or cookie sheets (depending on how you want to shape and bake the loaves). Divide the dough in half and form two loaves — using whatever shaping method you like (see page 43). Place in the prepared pans, cover and let rise again, until not quite double — about 30 minutes.

Preheat the oven to 375°F (190°C).

Place loaves in the oven and bake for 35 to 40 minutes, until loaves are golden brown and sound hollow when you tap them with your finger. Let cool on a rack for at least a little while.

Makes 2 loaves.

Yeast — a Matter of Life or Death

Up until now, the subject of baking has been a relatively simple matter. You mix up a bunch of ingredients, put the mixture in a pan, bake it. Pretty straightforward business.

With yeast, things get a bit weird, because yeast is no mere ingredient. It is a living organism. Like a hamster, it requires care and feeding or else it will die. Creepy? Sure, a little. But that's what makes yeast so interesting.

The most convenient way to purchase baking yeast is as a dry, granular product. This is called active dry yeast. Active because it's still alive — just dehydrated. Add liquid and warmth and the yeast begins to grow, exhaling, as a side effect, carbon dioxide, which creates the little bubbles you see in a loaf of bread.

The type of yeast recommended for the recipes in this book is quick-rise instant yeast. This product is an extra-speedy breed of yeast, which can be mixed directly into the dry ingredients in the recipe. It works much more quickly to rise bread dough than does ordinary yeast. Especially handy if you are an impatient person or in a big hurry for pizza. Purists may frown at this high-speed superyeast, but frankly, it's nobody's business.

You can also use regular, slow-speed active dry yeast in any of the recipes in this book that call for yeast. But you'll need to dissolve it in liquid before you add it to the flour, and the rising time of the dough will be considerably longer. (See page 51 for more details.)

Both kinds of active dry yeast are available in individual premeasured packets or in small cans or jars. If you do a lot of baking, a jar of yeast granules is more economical. But if you only use yeast once in a blue moon, the packets may be more convenient.

Molasses

Molasses is a liquid sweetener made from sugarcane (just like regular sugar). Depending on the process used to make it, molasses can be any color from medium brown to jet black. Generally, the darker the color, the stronger the taste, but even a light molasses will have a very distinctive flavor. So if you like it, use it. If not, then substitute another liquid sweetener, such as honey or maple syrup or corn syrup. It will bake just fine.

Wonderful White Bread

Wonderful Whole Wheat

Substitute 2 cups (500 ml) — or more — of whole wheat flour for the same amount of the all-purpose flour in the recipe. The more whole wheat flour you add in proportion to white flour, the heavier the resulting bread will be — so it's wise to experiment with gradual changes to the recipe until you find what you like best.

This is white bread you can feel really good about. Because you made it yourself. Awesome.

6 cups	(1.5 liters)	all-purpose flour (approximately), divided
3 tbsp.	(45 ml)	granulated sugar
4½ tsp.	(22 ml)	(2 envelopes) quick-rise instant yeast
2 tsp.	(10 ml)	salt
1½ cups	(375 ml)	water
½ cup	(125 ml)	milk
2 tbsp.	(30 ml)	butter or vegetable oil

In a large bowl, stir together 2 cups (500 ml) of the flour (only part of the total amount), the sugar, yeast granules and salt.

In a saucepan, or in a microwave-safe bowl, combine the water, milk and butter or oil. Heat on the stove or in the microwave until very warm to the touch — don't boil. Add warm liquid to the flour mixture, stirring to make a very gooey batter. Add the remaining flour, 1 cup at a time, stirring until the mixture becomes a soft, sticky dough that is difficult to stir. Dump it onto a well-floured surface and knead by hand, sprinkling with additional flour whenever necessary, until it is smooth and elastic and no longer sticky. This should take 8 to 10 minutes. You might not need to add the full amount of flour.

Place the dough in an oiled bowl that's large enough for the dough to expand, and turn it over to grease the top of the dough. Cover with a damp towel or plastic wrap and place in a warm spot to rise until doubled in size — about 30 to 45 minutes (see page 35).

When the dough has risen to double in size, punch it down, then knead it a few times on a floured surface. Let the dough rest while you prepare the baking pans.

Grease two 9 x 5-inch (23 x 13 cm) loaf pans. Divide the dough in half, form into two loaves (see page 35) and place the loaves in the pans to rise again — this time to almost (but not quite) double — about 30 minutes.

Preheat the oven to 400°F (200°C).

Place the risen loaves in the oven and bake for 25 to 30 minutes, or until the loaves are nicely browned on top and make a hollow sound when you tap them. Remove from pans and don't you dare taste them until completely cool. Ha! Like you could resist.

Makes 2 gorgeous loaves of bread.

Cinnamon Swirl Bread

Best — Breakfast — Toast — Ever.

In a small bowl, mix ¼ cup (60 ml) granulated sugar with 1 tbsp. (15 ml) cinnamon. Prepare the dough for Wonderful White Bread and let it rise once. Punch down the dough and divide it in half. Working with one half at a time, roll it out on a lightly floured surface to an 8 x 10-inch (20 x 25 cm) rectangle. Brush the surface lightly with water to moisten, then sprinkle with half the cinnamon mixture. Roll up tightly and place in a greased loaf pan, seam-side-down. Repeat with the remaining dough and cinnamon sugar. Let rise and bake as usual.

If you happen to be a raisin lover, you can also scatter a few raisins on top of the cinnamon sugar sprinkle before rolling up the dough. Most definitely excellent.

Multigrain Bread

Cheerfully wholesome, this bread is especially delicious toasted for breakfast.

Finishing Touches

Just before placing your loaves in the oven, brush the tops with a little beaten egg or milk, sprinkle with a few flakes of rolled oats or some seeds and make 3 diagonal slashes across the top of each loaf with a very sharp knife (for that oh-so-professional look).

1 cup	(250 ml)	water
1 cup	(250 ml)	buttermilk or plain yogurt
¼ cup	(60 ml)	butter or vegetable oil
½ cup	(125 ml)	quick-cooking rolled oats (not instant)
⅓ cup	(75 ml)	wheat germ
⅓ cup	(75 ml)	natural bran (not bran cereal)
5½ cups	(1.25 liters)	all-purpose flour (approximately), divided
¼ cup	(60 ml)	brown sugar
4½ tsp.	(22 ml)	(2 envelopes) quick-rise instant yeast
2 tsp.	(10 ml)	salt
1		egg, beaten

In a saucepan, or in a microwave-safe bowl, combine the water, buttermilk or yogurt and butter or oil. Heat on the stove or in the microwave until very warm to the touch — don't boil. Stir in the oats, wheat germ and bran, and set aside while you organize the rest of the ingredients for the recipe (or run out and buy the stuff you forgot).

In a large bowl, combine 1 cup (250 ml) of the flour, the brown sugar, yeast granules and salt. Add the warm liquid mixture and the egg, and stir to mix. Using a wooden spoon, continue to stir, adding the remaining flour, ½ cup (125 ml) at a time, until it forms a soft dough. Turn out onto a floured surface and knead by hand, sprinkling with additional flour as needed just until the dough is smooth and elastic, and no longer sticky. This should take about 6 to 8 minutes. You might not need to use all the flour.

Place the dough in an oiled bowl, and turn the dough over so all the sides are oiled. Cover with a damp towel or plastic wrap and let rise in a warm place until doubled in size — 30 to 40 minutes. (See rising instructions on page 35.)

When the dough has risen to double in volume, punch it down to deflate it, knead it a few times and let it rest while you prepare the baking pans.

Grease two 9 x 5-inch (23 x 13 cm) loaf pans. Divide the dough in half and form into two loaves (see instructions on page 43). Let rise again until almost double — about 30 minutes.

Preheat the oven to 375°F (190°C).

Place the loaves in the oven and bake for 25 to 30 minutes, or until they are nicely browned on top and sound hollow when you tap on them. Remove from pans and let cool on a rack before devouring. If you can wait that long.

Makes 2 loaves.

Variations

Whole Wheat Multigrain Bread
Substitute 1 to 2 cups (250 to 500 ml) whole wheat flour for the same quantity of all-purpose flour in the recipe. The more whole wheat flour you use, the denser the bread will be — so experiment gradually until you know what you like best.

Oatmeal Raisin Multigrain Bread
Omit the wheat germ and bran, and increase the oats to 1⅔ cups (400 ml). Soak ½ cup (125 ml) raisins in boiling water for 10 minutes, then drain and stir into the dough along with the egg.

Multiseed Multigrain Bread
Stir in 1 tbsp. (15 ml) each flaxseed, poppy seed and sunflower seed when you're mixing the dough.

Kneading Dough

Okay, you've mixed up the dough — so far, so good. Now you have to knead it. Right. Like what's that supposed to mean? Relax — it's fun.

First — a little background. When you look closely at a slice of bread, you'll notice that it consists of a bunch of bubbles in a fibrous framework. The fiber is called gluten — a stretchy protein that occurs in many grains, including wheat (from which most bread is made). Without gluten, the little bubbles that give bread its soft and spongy texture would have nothing to hold them together. The bread would have no structure and turn out dense and flat — and not in a good way either. Probably not what you had in mind.

   But gluten doesn't just happen. You have to develop it. That's where kneading comes in. When you work dough by hand (or with a mixer or other machine), you encourage the strands of gluten to become long and elastic so that they can contain the bubbles of carbon dioxide that the yeast exhales as it grows and so that your bread can rise beautifully (see page 35).

The beginner's method

Dust your work surface liberally with flour. Dump the dough onto this floured surface and dust the top with more flour. Press down on the dough, flattening it out in a pizza shape about 1 inch (2 cm) in thickness. Fold it into quarters. Flatten again as before. Fold again. Continue to flatten and fold, dusting the dough with as much flour as is necessary to keep the dough from sticking to the table or your hands. Keep going. Don't stop. Flatten, fold, flatten, fold, dust, and so on. Eventually the dough will become smooth and elastic and will no longer stick to the table or your hands. Keep kneading a little longer. When the dough feels very much like your earlobe (pinch it to find out), it's ready. There. Now, wasn't that fun?

Advanced transcendental kneading

After you've gained some bread-baking experience, you'll become so good at kneading that you'll no longer have to consciously flatten the dough and fold it into quarters. Instead, you'll use the heel of one hand to press down on the dough while turning it over with the other. It becomes rhythmic. Hypnotic. Transcendental. You become one with the dough as the squishy lump absorbs all your frustration and stress. You achieve inner peace. At the same time, you have made bread. I mean, is that perfect or what?

Loafing Around

When it comes to forming a loaf of bread, you have choices! You can simply form your dough into a regular loaf — squarish, baked in a loaf pan — which is convenient for sandwiches. Or you can make a fancy braided loaf. Or a round one. Or do something weird and free-form. Go ahead — loaf around.

Regular loaf

On a lightly floured surface, flatten the dough out with a rolling pin or by hand, to a 9-inch (23 cm) square. Approximately. Now roll the dough up firmly into a cylinder, pressing out any air pockets or bubbles. Place in a well-greased 9 x 5-inch (23 x 13 cm) loaf pan and tuck the ends under neatly. There. Nice and tidy. Let rise and then bake.

Rustic round loaf

By hand, form the dough into an evenly rounded ball and place it — smooth-side-up — on a well-greased baking sheet that has been lightly sprinkled with cornmeal. Cover with plastic wrap or a damp cloth and let rise until almost (but not quite) doubled. Just before baking, remove the cover and cut a shallow X in the top of the loaf with a very sharp knife. When the loaf is baked, this cut will allow the loaf to expand, giving it a very snazzy, professional look.

Beautiful braided loaf

For a simple braided loaf, divide the dough into three equal pieces. Roll each piece into a long rope, about 1 inch (2 cm) thick. Pinch the three ropes together at one end and proceed to braid the three strands until you come to the end. Pinch the other end together so it doesn't unravel and place the braid on a well-greased baking sheet.

For a double-decker braided loaf, you can make two braids — the smaller one on top of the larger one. Simply divide the original lump of dough into two unequal portions (one noticeably larger than the other). Divide each into three ropes, then braid each one as above. Place the smaller braid on top of the larger braid, let rise and bake as usual. There: double-decker!

Crazy mixed-up loaves

Make a loaf out of balls of dough squashed into any shape of pan. Roll the dough out into a long snake and form it into a spiral, a squiggle, an octopus, a figure eight. Make a turtle, a bunny, an elephant. Shape your dough into an alligator. A dump truck. A daisy. Have fun. Go crazy. It'll all get eaten in the end.

Roll 'Em

A dinner roll is nothing more than a teensy loaf of bread. Use any bread dough recipe and make a batch of dinner rolls instead of the usual loaf. They'll bake in about half the time (or less) of a full-size loaf.

Plain Round Rolls

Form the dough into evenly rounded balls, 2 inches (5 cm) across. Place on a well-greased baking sheet or in the cups of a well-greased muffin pan. Let rise and bake.

Plain round rolls

Cloverleaf Rolls

Pinch off 1-inch (2 cm) balls of dough, and place 3 of them into each cup of a well-greased muffin pan. Let rise and bake.

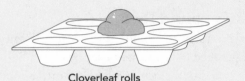

Cloverleaf rolls

Knots

Roll pieces of dough into ropes — about ½ inch (1 cm) thick and 6 inches (15 cm) long. Tie into a loose knot and place on a well-greased baking sheet, with one end sticking out of the top and the other one tucked underneath. Let rise and bake.

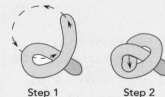

Step 1   Step 2

Crescents

With a rolling pin on a lightly floured surface, roll the dough out into a circle, about 12 inches (30 cm) in diameter. Brush the entire surface lightly with melted butter. Cut into 8 to 12 wedges pizzawise. Working with one wedge at a time, starting from the outside edge, roll the dough inward toward the point, then place on a well-greased baking sheet and bend lightly to form a crescent. (Make sure to place the crescents on the baking sheet with the point-side-down to prevent unraveling.) Let rise, then bake. *Ta-da!*

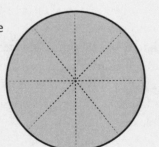

Awesome Egg Challah

This traditional bread is so stunning that it would still be worth making even if it didn't taste so wonderful.

4 cups	(1 liter)	all-purpose flour (approximately), divided
4½ tsp.	(22 ml)	(2 envelopes) quick-rise instant yeast
¼ cup	(60 ml)	granulated sugar or honey
2 tsp.	(10 ml)	salt
1 cup	(250 ml)	hot tap water
½ cup	(125 ml)	vegetable oil
2		eggs, lightly beaten
		poppy seeds or sesame seeds for sprinkling

In a very large bowl, stir together 2 cups (500 ml) of the flour, the yeast, sugar or honey and salt. Add the hot water, the oil and the eggs, and beat with a wooden spoon until smooth. Gradually add the additional flour, ½ cup (125 ml) at a time, until the dough becomes too stiff to stir. It will still be sticky. Dump the dough onto a well-floured surface and knead until smooth, elastic and feels damp, but no longer sticks to your hands or the table. (See page 42 for all the gory details on kneading.) You might not need to use all the flour.

Grease a large bowl and place the dough in it, then turn it over to grease all sides. Cover bowl with plastic wrap and put in a warm place to rise until doubled in volume — about 30 to 45 minutes.

Punch down the dough, turn it out onto a floured surface and knead it a few times. Form into one large braided loaf (see directions on page 43) and place on a well-greased baking sheet. Cover with plastic wrap or a damp cloth and put back in a warm spot to rise until nearly (but not quite) doubled — 20 to 30 minutes.

Preheat the oven to 375°F (190°C).

Brush loaf with an egg wash glaze (see sidebar) and sprinkle with poppy seeds or sesame seeds, if desired. Place in the preheated oven and bake for 30 to 35 minutes, or until the bread is dark golden brown and sounds hollow when you tap it with a finger.

Let cool (for at least a little while) before serving.

Makes 1 awesome challah.

Egg Wash Glaze

In a small bowl, whisk 1 egg yolk with 1 tbsp. (15 ml) water. Use this mixture to brush the top of challah or any other bread where you want a shiny, golden brown crust. Gorgeous!

Whole Wheat Positive
You can substitute whole wheat flour for all or part of the all-purpose flour in this recipe. Start with a small proportion, and if you like the result, you can use more whole wheat flour next time.

Italian Everything Dough

Need pizza?

Start with a batch of Italian Everything Dough. Then keep going:

Preheat the oven to 425°F (220°C). Cut the dough in half. Roll each half out into a 12-inch (30 cm) circle and place on an oiled pizza pan lightly sprinkled with cornmeal. Pinch the edges up slightly. Spread the dough evenly with tomato sauce, cheese, pepperoni, mushrooms, peppers, anchovies (you know the drill). Bake for 20 to 25 minutes, until the crust is browned underneath and the cheese is melted.

Makes two 12-inch (30 cm) pizzas.

You can use this dough to make your own homemade pizza or the best focaccia you have ever tasted. Or both.

3½ cups	(800 ml)	all-purpose flour (approximately), divided
2¼ tsp.	(11 ml)	(1 envelope) quick-rise instant yeast
1 tsp.	(5 ml)	salt
1 cup	(250 ml)	hot tap water
¼ cup	(60 ml)	olive oil or vegetable oil

In a large bowl, stir together 2 cups (500 ml) of the flour, the yeast granules and the salt. Add the hot water and oil, and stir until the mixture is smooth (it will be sticky and gooey —that's fine). Now add the remaining flour, ½ cup (125 ml) at a time, stirring it with a wooden spoon until it becomes too sticky to stir.

At this point, dump about ½ cup (125 ml) of the flour onto a work surface, spread it around a bit, then turn the sticky lump of dough out onto this floured surface. Begin kneading the dough by hand, adding only as much additional flour as is necessary to keep it from sticking to your hands (or the table). Continue to knead for 8 to 10 minutes, or until the dough is smooth and elastic. You might not need to use all the flour.

Place the dough in an oiled bowl. Turn the dough over to make sure all the sides are oiled, then cover with plastic wrap and place in a warm spot to rise until doubled in volume — about 30 minutes (see rising suggestions — page 35).

When the dough has doubled, punch it down to deflate it, then knead it a few times on a lightly floured surface. Let rest for 5 minutes and then use as a base for pizza or to make some Fabulous Focaccia (see page 47).

Makes enough dough for two 8 or 9-inch (20 or 23 cm) Fabulous Focaccia breads or two 12-inch (30 cm) pizzas.

Whole Wheat Positive
You can substitute whole wheat flour for all or part of the all-purpose flour in this recipe. Start with a small proportion, and if you like the result, you can use more whole wheat flour next time.

Fabulous Focaccia

Start with one recipe of Italian Everything Dough. Add inspiration. Bake until delicious.

Prepare Italian Everything Dough. Let the dough rise once, punch it down, then let it rest for 5 minutes while you prepare the baking pans. Cut the dough in half and roll each half out to fit into a greased 8 or 9-inch (20 or 23 cm) round cake pan or on cookie sheets.

Top with whatever weird and wonderful toppings you like (inspirations follow), cover loosely with plastic wrap and let rise again until puffed to almost double — about 20 to 30 minutes.

Preheat the oven to 375°F (190°C).

Place focaccia in the oven and bake for 25 to 30 minutes, until the dough is lightly browned on the edges and the center is no longer gooey (stick a fork into it to check).

Just try to resist eating the whole thing immediately.

Makes 2 fabulous 8 or 9-inch (20 or 23 cm) focaccias.

Focaccia Inspirations

Each of the following combinations is enough to top one 8 or 9-inch (20 or 23 cm) round focaccia. Feel free to ignore these suggestions completely.

Mainly Mediterranean

¼ cup	(60 ml)	chopped brine-cured olives
¼ cup	(60 ml)	chopped sundried tomatoes
½ cup	(125 ml)	crumbled feta cheese
		salt, pepper and crumbled rosemary

Somewhat Sicilian

1		onion, sliced and sautéed in olive oil
1		small ripe tomato, coarsely chopped
¼ cup	(60 ml)	grated Parmesan cheese
		salt, pepper and crumbled oregano

Perfectly Pesto

¼ cup	(60 ml)	prepared pesto sauce
¼ cup	(60 ml)	chopped sundried tomatoes
½ cup	(125 ml)	crumbled goat cheese

Not Quite Naked

2 tbsp.	(30 ml)	olive oil
2		cloves garlic, chopped
		salt, pepper and crumbled rosemary

The Truth About Gluten

Gluten is a stretchy protein found in wheat and other grains, such as oats and rye. This is what gives bread its spongy texture and allows a loaf of bread to hold itself up as it rises. When we knead the dough, we develop the gluten structure, causing the fibers to stretch and strengthen. In bread, this is a good thing. So flour with a high gluten content — made from "hard wheat" — is best for that purpose.

Flour made from "soft wheat" has a lower gluten content and is best for baking more delicate things, such as pastries and light cakes. You're looking for fluffy and fragile, rather than sturdy and chewy.

All-purpose flour is somewhere in between on the gluten scale. It has enough gluten to make a decent loaf of bread, but is still fine for baking cakes and pastries. Most of the recipes in this book call for all-purpose flour.

Some people can't tolerate any gluten whatsoever in their diet and have to avoid all foods that contain wheat, rye, barley, oats and various other grains. Some recipes in this book are gluten-free or can be made gluten-free with specific ingredient substitutions, such as commercially produced gluten-free flour, ground nuts, potato starch or rice flour. So go ahead and experiment — you may just invent something wonderful!

Universal Sweet Dough

One batch of this dough will make two pans of Cinnamon Buns (or variations thereof) or two Bubble Breads. Or make one of each! Perfect if you can't decide what you want.

4 cups	**(1 liter)**	**all-purpose flour (approximately), divided**
⅓ cup	**(75 ml)**	**granulated sugar**
4½ tsp.	**(22 ml)**	**(2 envelopes) quick-rise instant yeast**
½ tsp.	**(2 ml)**	**salt**
¾ cup	**(175 ml)**	**milk**
½ cup	**(125 ml)**	**water**
⅓ cup	**(75 ml)**	**butter**
2		**eggs, lightly beaten**

In a large bowl, stir together 2 cups (500 ml) of the flour (this is only part of the total amount of flour) with the sugar, yeast and salt.

In a saucepan, or in a microwave-safe bowl, combine the milk, water and butter. Heat on the stove or in the microwave until very warm to the touch — don't boil. Add warm liquid to the flour mixture and beat with an electric mixer, or by hand with a sturdy spoon, until the mixture forms a stringy, sticky, gooey batter. Beat in the eggs, one at a time, and then add the remaining flour ½ cup (125 ml) at a time, mixing well, until the dough becomes too difficult to stir.

Now dump the dough out onto a well-floured surface and knead by hand for 6 to 8 minutes, sprinkling lightly with additional flour to keep the dough from sticking to your hands or the table. (You might not need to use the entire amount of flour.) Once the dough is no longer sticky and feels like a damp earlobe when you pinch it, it's ready to rise. Place it in an oiled bowl, and turn it over to oil the top. Cover with plastic wrap, place in a warm spot (see rising suggestions — page 35) and let rise until doubled in volume — about 30 to 40 minutes.

Punch the dough down to deflate it, knead it a few times and it's ready to shape into any of the following incredibly easy, but very impressive, creations.

Whole Wheat Positive

You can substitute whole wheat flour for all or part of the all-purpose flour in this recipe. Start with a small proportion, and if you like the result, you can use more whole wheat flour next time.

Cinnamon Buns

One recipe of Universal Sweet Dough will make two pans of either Cinnamon Buns or any of the variations that follow. Bake both now or bake one and freeze the other, unbaked, to enjoy on a rainy day.

1 recipe		**Universal Sweet Dough (page 49)**
1 cup	**(250 ml)**	**brown sugar**
2 tsp.	**(10 ml)**	**cinnamon**
½ cup	**(125 ml)**	**butter, softened**
½ cup	**(125 ml)**	**raisins or dried cranberries**
		Shiny Sugar Glaze (page 173)

Prepare the Universal Sweet Dough according to the recipe. Let it rise once, punch it down and set it aside to rest while you gather up the filling ingredients.

In a small bowl, combine the brown sugar and the cinnamon. Have ready the softened butter and raisins or cranberries. Grease an 8 or 9-inch (20 or 23 cm) square baking pan.

Divide the dough in half. Working with one half at a time, roll the dough out with a rolling pin on a lightly floured surface to form a rectangle approximately 9 x 12 inches (23 x 30 cm) in size. Spread the surface as evenly as possible with half of the softened butter. Sprinkle with half of the cinnamon-sugar mixture and half of the raisins or cranberries. Starting with a short side, roll the dough up as tightly as possible into a sausage shape and pinch the ends together to keep it from unraveling. With a sharp knife, cut crosswise into 9 equal slices and arrange them, cut-side-up, in the prepared baking pan. Repeat with the remaining dough and the remaining filling ingredients. (If you're freezing some of the buns to bake later, see page 51 for directions.)

Cover pans with plastic wrap, place in a warm spot to rise (see rising suggestions — page 35) and let rise until nearly doubled (about 30 minutes).

Preheat the oven to 375°F (190°C).

Bake for 25 to 30 minutes, or until buns are nicely browned on top and sound hollow when you tap them with your finger. Drizzle with Shiny Sugar Glaze (page 173) and let cool before devouring.

Makes 2 pans of Cinnamon Buns, about 9 buns in each pan.

Supersticky Variation

In a small saucepan, combine 1 cup (250 ml) each of butter, brown sugar and coarsely chopped pecans or walnuts. Place over medium heat and cook, stirring, until the butter is melted and the mixture is gooey. Spread half of this mixture in the bottom of each prepared baking pan.

Prepare the Cinnamon Buns (page 50) and arrange the unbaked buns on top of the buttery sugary mixture. Cover, let rise and bake as for regular Cinnamon Buns. When they are baked, turn them upside-down to remove from the pan. Gooey sticky deliciousness.

Deadly Chocolate Variation

Instead of using cinnamon-sugar as a filling, spread the rolled-out dough with about ⅓ cup (75 ml) of chocolate fudge sauce (good-quality store-bought ice cream sauce from a jar is fine), and sprinkle evenly with about ½ cup (125 ml) semisweet chocolate chips. Roll up, cut into slices and arrange in baking pans as for Cinnamon Buns.

Cover, let rise and bake as for the regular Cinnamon Buns. Except, they're not. For total chocolate overload, drizzle with Chocolate Ganache Glaze (page 171).

To Freeze for a Rainy Day

Prepare Cinnamon Buns (page 50) and arrange them in a well-greased disposable foil pan (or in a pan that you can live without while it's in the freezer) — but do not let them rise. Wrap well in foil or plastic wrap, and place in an airtight plastic bag, sealed with tape or a twist tie so that the dough won't be exposed to dry freezer air. Place in the freezer.

When you want to bake, remove the frozen pan from the freezer and unwrap it. Cover loosely with plastic wrap and let thaw at room temperature. Once the buns are fully thawed, they will slowly begin to rise. Let them rise until nearly doubled in volume. It should take 2 to 3 hours from the time you take the pan out of the freezer until the buns are ready to go into the oven. Bake as usual.

Slow Yeast

Because we're impatient, we specify that you use quick-rise instant yeast in all the yeast bread recipes in this book. It activates quickly and is easy to work with. But if you prefer, you can use regular active dry yeast granules instead. The rising time will be longer and you'll need to dilute the yeast with water before mixing into the dough, but otherwise it's just fine. Here's how to use it:

Pour ½ cup (125 ml) of the total amount of warm water in the recipe into a small bowl. Sprinkle in the dry yeast granules. Let stand for 5 to 10 minutes. The yeast will begin to bubble and foam in a quite interesting way. Stir to mix, then add to the dry ingredients along with the remaining liquid. Proceed with the recipe as usual. You can expect the rising time to be considerably longer than for quick-rise yeast — as much as double the time, in fact.

Bubble Bread

One batch of Universal Sweet Dough will make two pans of this fun bread. Bake one for brunch today — freeze the other to bake next week. Or make one Bubble Bread, using half the dough and half the ingredients below, and make Cinnamon Buns with the other half.

1 recipe		**Universal Sweet Dough**
1½ cups	**(375 ml)**	**granulated sugar**
1 tbsp.	**(15 ml)**	**cinnamon**
1 cup	**(250 ml)**	**butter, melted**
1 cup	**(250 ml)**	**raisins**
1 cup	**(250 ml)**	**chopped walnuts or pecans**

Prepare the Universal Sweet Dough according to the recipe (page 49). Let it rise once, punch it down and set it aside to rest while you gather up the filling ingredients.

In a small bowl, stir together the sugar and cinnamon. Have ready the melted butter, the raisins and the nuts.

Grease two 9 or 10-inch (23 or 25 cm) bundt or tube pans.

Divide the dough in half. Working with one half at a time, pinch off pieces of dough, about 1 inch (2 cm) across, and roll by hand into small balls. One at a time, dunk each ball in the melted butter, then roll it in the cinnamon-sugar. Arrange in a prepared pan. When you have a full layer of dough balls, sprinkle with some of the raisins and nuts. Continue adding balls and sprinkling nuts and raisins until you've used half of the sugar, raisins and nuts.

Repeat this process with the remaining dough (and all the rest of the sugar, nuts and raisins), or use the remaining dough to make Cinnamon Buns. Decisions, decisions.

Cover and let rise until almost doubled — about 30 minutes. (See rising suggestions — page 35.)

Preheat the oven to 375°F (190°C).

Place Bubble Bread in the oven and bake for 30 to 35 minutes, until golden brown. Invert the pan and remove Bubble Bread to a rack to cool. A drizzle of Shiny Sugar Glaze (page 173) is a nice (but optional) finishing touch.

Makes 2 very nifty Bubble Breads.

Clueless Troubleshooting: Quick Breads and Yeast Breads

Okay, so your bread didn't turn out so well. It's as dense as a doorstop and tastes like, well, you don't actually know because you'd need a chain saw to cut it. Relax — we've all been there. All of the following problems have been experienced by ordinary persons (such as yourself), many of whom have gone on to live perfectly normal lives. And yes, to bake bread again.

Quick Breads

It didn't rise at all.

✓ Did you remember to add the baking powder or baking soda? That's pretty important.

✓ Is your baking powder or baking soda fresh — or has it been in your cupboard for five years? Or is it the old box you used to deodorize the refrigerator? Treat yourself to a new box — you deserve it.

✓ Did you let the batter sit around for a long time? Baking soda and baking powder begin working as soon as the liquid has been added and the batter is mixed. With time, the batter can lose its get-up-and-go. Get up and get it into the oven more quickly next time.

It rose nicely, then collapsed.

✓ Was your quick bread fully baked when you took it out of the oven? Are you sure? Do the toothpick test next time (see page 23).

✓ Did you open the oven door more than was absolutely necessary? Don't. When you let the heat out of the oven, it can make a quick bread cranky and cause it to collapse.

Ack! My bread is lopsided!

✓ Your oven may not heat evenly, causing one part to be hotter than another. Turning the baking pans around midway through the baking time may help avoid lopsidedness. Move the pans

back to front and switch oven racks. This may not totally cure the problem, but could reduce it. But work quickly (see previous answer to collapsing).
✓ Are your oven racks flat? Check them. If the baking pan is on a slant, your bread will be too.

The bottom burned before the bread was done.
✓ If your oven heats unevenly, try using a higher rack to bake next time. Or simply lower the heat by 10 to 25 degrees.
✓ Get an oven thermometer and use it to check if your oven is behaving itself. If the temperature is too high (or too low), you can either compensate by lowering or raising the temperature control, or get your oven recalibrated by a repairperson.

The batter overflowed the pan!
✓ Did you use the correct size pan for the recipe? Check the volume of the baking pan or measure the diameter to make sure it's what you need.
✓ Or maybe you added too much baking powder or baking soda.

The breads look fine, but they have a weird taste.
✓ If you didn't mix your dry ingredients thoroughly, you may have lumps of baking soda or baking powder, which can give baked goods an icky, metallic flavor. Be sure to mix (or even sift) the dry ingredients together before adding the liquids.
✓ Have your ingredients gone bad? Nothing can disguise the taste of stale nuts or whole wheat flour or rancid oil. The off flavor will permeate everything and make even the most wonderful loaf of bread taste terrible. Buy fresh ingredients and store them in the refrigerator or freezer.

Yeast Breads

The yeast bread didn't rise at all.

✓ Dead yeast. Maybe it died of old age. (Was it in your cupboard for a few years?) Maybe it died in the store before you even bought it. (It happens sometimes.) Either way, you'll have to buy a fresh package. Or maybe you killed it (you fiend!) by adding liquid that was too hot. Try again and be more careful next time.

✓ Cold dough. Was your rising spot too cool? Try warming up the dough by placing the bowl on a heating pad or in a larger bowl filled with warm water, and give it a bit more time to rise.

The dough didn't rise enough.

✓ Low-gluten flour — such as cake and pastry flour — won't develop the proper stretchy framework that allows a yeast bread to hold its shape. It's like trying to construct an apartment building out of applesauce. Use all-purpose or high-gluten bread flour.

✓ The dough may have been just too heavy. Too many whole grains or other additions (raisins, seeds, cracked wheat, oats and so on) will keep bread dough from rising sufficiently. Poor thing just can't lift itself up. Cut back on the "stuff" or learn to enjoy dense bread.

It rose, then collapsed.

✓ Your rising spot may have been too warm, causing your dough to rise too quickly and overstretch itself. Find a slightly cooler spot next time.

✓ Did you let the dough rise too long? If you allow yeast dough to overrise, it simply can't support itself and will collapse. So if you can't bake your bread when it's ready to go into the oven, you will need to buy yourself some time. Punch down the dough, cover it and refrigerate to slow the rising process. Remove from refrigerator when you have time to let it finish rising and bake. An extra rise doesn't hurt either — it develops flavor and refines the texture.

The bread browned too quickly.

✓ Your oven is too hot. Don't feel bad — it happens to even the nicest ovens. Check the temperature with an oven thermometer and either adjust the controls to compensate (lower the temperature by 10 to 25 degrees) or call a repairperson to recalibrate the thermostat.

✓ You may have had too much sugar (or honey or other sweetener) in your dough. Reduce the amount of sweetener next time.

✓ Did you glaze the top of the bread with egg wash? It can cause the bread to get really brown. Omit the glaze next time — or learn to appreciate the effect.

The loaf didn't brown enough.

✓ The oven isn't hot enough. Check the temperature with an oven thermometer to make sure the temperature is accurate. If necessary, you can raise the oven temperature by 10 to 25 degrees to compensate. Or get the oven repaired.

✓ Use an egg wash glaze next time. It will give you a darker crust.

My bread looks like Swiss cheese.

✓ Your bread rose too quickly, Maybe your rising spot is too warm. Find another place.

✓ The dough wasn't punched down enough, leaving big air pockets in it. Next time you make bread, knead it for a couple of minutes after punching it down, to eliminate big bubbles.

My free-form loaves look like giant pancakes!

✓ Your shaped dough rose too long before baking. It got tired and could no longer hold itself up in a nice loafy shape. Next time, put the shaped loaves in the oven before they have fully doubled in size. They will continue to rise there.

✓ The dough was too soft. If you're planning to bake a free-form loaf, make a slightly stiffer dough by kneading in a little extra flour. The dough will hold its shape better and not spread out as much.

The top of the bread split.

✓ Hey, it happens. Next time, avoid unsightly splits by taking a very sharp knife (or utility blade) and making a few preemptive slashes in the top of the unbaked loaf just before it goes in the oven. You'll still have splits, but at least they'll be pretty ones.

The bread was overdone on top but underdone on the bottom (or vice versa).

✓ Check your oven temperature with an oven thermometer. If the oven is too hot, the outsides of the bread will look done before the insides are properly baked. Adjust the temperature to compensate for this.

✓ The heat in your oven may be uneven. Place loaves on a lower shelf if the top is browning too quickly or on a higher shelf if the bottom is burning.

Muffins and Biscuits

They go with coffee. They go with soup. They can go it alone. Butter them or don't. Spread them with cream cheese or strawberry jam. Eat them plain. In a car. On a bus. At the breakfast table. A batch of freshly baked muffins or biscuits can turn a panful of carelessly scrambled eggs into a perfectly respectable brunch, or a bowl of leftover chili into a two-course dinner.

Muffins

Beautiful Buttermilk Muffins

Start with a basic buttermilk muffin — and have your way with it. Add blueberries or poppy seeds or chocolate chips. In fact, you can add just about anything you like! Muffins are so personal, don't you think?

1 cup	(250 ml)	buttermilk, thinned yogurt or sour milk (see page 26)
¾ cup	(175 ml)	granulated sugar
½ cup	(125 ml)	vegetable oil
2		eggs
1 tsp.	(5 ml)	vanilla extract or grated lemon zest
2 cups	(500 ml)	all-purpose flour
2 tsp.	(10 ml)	baking powder
½ tsp.	(2 ml)	baking soda

Preheat the oven to 375°F (190°C). Grease a 12-cup muffin pan or line with paper liners.

In large bowl, whisk together the sugar, oil, eggs and vanilla or lemon zest until light(ish).

In another bowl, mix the flour, baking powder and baking soda. Add this mixture to the egg mixture, in two or three portions, alternating with the buttermilk (or whatever you're using) and stirring to mix after each addition. Beat only until combined — don't overbeat! Spoon the batter into the prepared muffin pan, filling each cup about ¾ full. Place in the oven and bake for 20 to 25 minutes, until lightly browned on top.

Makes 12 muffins.

Whole Wheat Positive
You can substitute whole wheat flour for all or part of the all-purpose flour in this recipe. Start with a small proportion, and if you like the result, you can use more whole wheat flour next time.

Variations on a Muffin

Blueberry Muffins

Prepare batter using lemon zest, not vanilla. Stir 1 cup (250 ml) fresh or frozen blueberries into the batter before spooning it into the muffin pan. (If using frozen berries, don't thaw them beforehand.) Bake as usual.

Chocolate Chip Muffins

Prepare batter using vanilla, not lemon zest. Stir 1 cup (250 ml) chocolate chips into the batter before spooning it into the muffin pan. Bake as usual.

Poppy Seed Muffins

Mix ¼ cup (60 ml) poppy seeds into the buttermilk and let soak while you gather the rest of the ingredients. Prepare batter with either vanilla or lemon zest, and add poppy seed mixture with the buttermilk. Bake as usual.

Cranberry or Cherry Muffins

Prepare batter with either lemon zest or vanilla. Stir 1 cup (250 ml) of chopped dried cranberries or dried cherries into the batter before baking. Bake as usual.

Oven Temperature — How Can We Be Sure?

In the bad old days, when your great-grandma baked a loaf of bread in her big old wood-fired cookstove, she probably just stuck her hand into the oven and could tell right away if it was hot enough. Fortunately for us, it's no longer necessary to risk second-degree burns just to bake a cake. We set the temperature on the oven and never give it another thought. But can we trust it? Maybe not.

Occasionally an oven will lie. So how do you know?

Well, your first clue is when your chocolate chip cookies burst into flames. But that's an extreme example. Most of the time the temperature will be just a little bit off. Your recipes will brown too quickly or the outsides will be done before the insides are fully baked. The bottoms of cakes or or cookies may burn or your piecrust may turn brown before the filling is cooked.

If you suspect that you're the victim of oven temperature fraud, buy yourself an inexpensive oven thermometer and use it to check. If you're oven is running too hot, set the dial to a lower temperature; if not hot enough, set it higher.

If all else fails, call your great-grandma. She'll know what to do.

Honey Bran Muffins

Measuring Honey or Molasses

Measuring honey, molasses or any other sticky liquid is a yucky, messy business. But not if you plan ahead. Before you pour the honey into the measuring cup, first measure any oil or melted butter you're using in the recipe. The oil leaves a film on the inside of the cup and the honey will then slide right out. If there's no oil in your recipe, you can lightly oil the cup or spray it with nonstick baking spray instead.

These excellent muffins will make you feel all kinds of virtuous and healthy. This is a good thing at breakfast time, because we all know it goes downhill from there.

½ cup	(125 ml)	vegetable oil
½ cup	(125 ml)	honey
1		egg
1 cup	(250 ml)	all-purpose flour
1 tsp.	(5 ml)	baking soda
1 cup	(250 ml)	buttermilk, thinned yogurt or sour milk (see page 26)
1½ cups	(375 ml)	natural bran (not bran cereal)
½ cup	(125 ml)	raisins (optional)

Preheat the oven to 375°F (190°C). Grease a 12-cup muffin pan or line with paper liners.

In a large bowl, whisk together the vegetable oil, honey and egg until smooth. In a small bowl, combine the flour with the baking soda. Add the flour mixture to the egg mixture in two or three portions, alternating with the buttermilk (or whatever you're using), stirring just until everything is evenly moistened. Stir in the bran and the raisins, if you're using them.

Spoon batter into the prepared muffin pan, filling the cups about ¾ full. Bake for 20 to 25 minutes, until a toothpick poked into the middle of a muffin comes out clean.

Makes 10 to 12 muffins.

Whole Wheat Positive
You can substitute whole wheat flour for all or part of the all-purpose flour in this recipe. Start with a small proportion, and if you like the result, you can use more whole wheat flour next time.

Blender Peanut Butter Muffins

Plain, chocolate chip or filled with jelly. A cold glass of milk is mandatory.

2 cups	**(500 ml)**	**all-purpose flour**
¼ cup	**(60 ml)**	**granulated sugar**
1 tsp.	**(5 ml)**	**baking powder**
½ tsp.	**(2 ml)**	**baking soda**
1 cup	**(250 ml)**	**creamy peanut butter**
1 cup	**(250 ml)**	**milk**
2		**eggs**
1 tsp.	**(5 ml)**	**vanilla**
1 cup	**(250 ml)**	**chocolate chips (optional)**

Preheat the oven to 400°F (200°C). Grease a 12-cup muffin pan or line with paper liners.

In a large bowl, stir together the flour, sugar, baking powder and baking soda.

In the container of a blender or food processor, combine the peanut butter, milk, eggs and vanilla. Blend or process until smooth. Add to the flour mixture, stirring just until everything is evenly moistened and combined.

Mix in the chocolate chips if you're using them, then spoon the batter into the prepared muffin pan, filling the cups about ¾ full. Bake for 15 to 20 minutes, until the muffins are lightly browned and a toothpick poked into the middle of a muffin comes out clean.

Makes about 12 muffins.

Whole Wheat Positive
You can substitute whole wheat flour for all or part of the all-purpose flour in this recipe. Start with a small proportion, and if you like the result, you can use more whole wheat flour next time.

What about peanut butter and jelly?

The classic combo in a muffin. Here's what you do. Omit the chocolate chips and fill each muffin cup ½ full. Place 1 tsp. (5 ml) of your favorite jam or jelly in the middle of each muffin, then add the remaining batter to cover. Bake as usual. Yum.

And if that isn't scrumptious enough ...

Top each unbaked muffin with a sprinkle of All-Purpose Crumble Topping (page 182). Bake muffins as if perfectly normal. Which they aren't, of course.

Oatmeal Raisin Muffins

Plump those raisins!

Instead of just tossing a bunch of raisins into the batter, why not plump them first? Don't be shy — it's not embarrassing. Here's what you do.

Measure your raisins into a bowl and cover them with boiling water. Let them sit while you prepare the rest of the recipe, then drain well and add them to whatever you're making. The raisins will come out soft and, well, plump. This is especially useful in recipes where the baking time is short (as for muffins) and the raisins wouldn't otherwise have much time to soften in the oven.

Purists may prefer to omit the raisins. That's fine. Or you can even substitute chocolate chips, if you're feeling wild and crazy.

1 cup	(250 ml)	quick-cooking rolled oats (not instant)
1 cup	(250 ml)	buttermilk, plain yogurt or sour milk (see page 26)
1		egg
⅓ cup	(75 ml)	brown sugar
¼ cup	(60 ml)	vegetable oil
1 cup	(250 ml)	all-purpose flour
1 tsp.	(5 ml)	baking powder
½ tsp.	(2 ml)	baking soda
½ cup	(125 ml)	raisins (or chocolate chips or nothing, optional)

Preheat the oven to 400°F (200°C). Grease a 12-cup muffin pan or line with paper liners.

In a bowl, stir together the rolled oats and the buttermilk (or whatever liquid you're using). Let soak for 10 minutes or so, then whisk in the egg, brown sugar and vegetable oil.

In another bowl, stir together the flour, baking powder and baking soda. Add this mixture to the oat mixture and stir just until combined. Add the raisins (or whatever) if you're using them. Spoon batter into the prepared muffin pan, filling the cups about ¾ full. Bake for 18 to 20 minutes, or until the tops spring back when you touch them and are lightly browned. Let cool slightly before serving (but they're really best while they're still warm).

Makes 9 to 10 muffins.

Whole Wheat Positive
You can substitute whole wheat flour for all or part of the all-purpose flour in this recipe. Start with a small proportion, and if you like the result, you can use more whole wheat flour next time.

Cranberry Cornmeal Muffins

You can omit the dried cranberries for a basic cornmeal muffin — to serve with a bowl of chili, for instance.

1½ cups	(375 ml)	all-purpose flour
1 cup	(250 ml)	yellow cornmeal
¼ cup	(60 ml)	granulated sugar
2 tbsp.	(30 ml)	baking powder
½ tsp.	(2 ml)	salt
¼ cup	(60 ml)	vegetable oil
1		egg
1⅓ cups	(325 ml)	milk
½ cup	(125 ml)	dried cranberries, halved (optional)

Don't leave your muffin cups empty

When there's not enough batter to fill all the cups in a muffin pan, fill the empty compartments with water. It will add a bit of humidity to the oven (a good thing) and prevent the pan from scorching.

Preheat the oven to 400° F (200° C). Grease a 12-cup muffin pan or line with paper liners.

In a large bowl, stir together the flour, cornmeal, sugar, baking powder and salt. In a smaller bowl, whisk together the oil, the egg and the milk. Add the milk mixture to the flour mixture and stir until combined. A few lumps are no big deal, so don't overbeat it. Stir in the chopped cranberries, if you're using them.

Spoon the batter into the prepared muffin pan, filling the cups about ¾ full. Bake for about 15 to 18 minutes, or until very lightly browned and the muffins spring back when you touch the tops. Remove from pan and serve warm.

Makes 10 to 12 large muffins, which really do lose some of their charm once they're cool.

Whole Wheat Positive
You can substitute whole wheat flour for all or part of the all-purpose flour in this recipe. Start with a small proportion, and if you like the result, you can use more whole wheat flour next time.

Gluten-Free Banana Muffins

*All bakers should have a few good gluten-free recipes in their repertoire —
and this is a delicious one. The muffins are light and fluffy, very banana-
ish and easy as anything.*

¾ cup	(175 ml)	brown rice flour
¼ cup	(60 ml)	cornstarch
2 tsp.	(10 ml)	baking powder
¼ tsp.	(1 ml)	salt
3		ripe bananas, well mashed
½ cup	(125 ml)	vegetable oil
½ cup	(125 ml)	granulated sugar
2		eggs
½ cup	(125 ml)	raisins, chocolate chips, blueberries, whatever

Preheat the oven to 375°F (190°C). Grease a 12-cup muffin pan or
line with paper liners.

In a small bowl, stir together the rice flour, cornstarch, baking
powder and salt. Set aside.

In a large bowl, beat together the mashed bananas, oil, sugar and
eggs with an electric mixer. Continue to beat this mixture on high
speed for 2 or 3 minutes, until quite fluffy. Add the flour mixture and
beat just until everything is combined. Stir in raisins, chips, berries
or whatever you're using. Spoon batter into the prepared muffin pan,
filling the cups nearly to the top. Bake for 20 to 25 minutes, until
muffins are lightly browned on top and a toothpick poked into the
middle of a muffin comes out clean.

Makes about 12 muffins.

Apple Granola Muffins

Apple-studded, not too sweet, nice and moist, these irresistible muffins make a great addition to breakfast or brunch.

½ cup	(125 ml)	all-purpose flour
½ cup	(125 ml)	whole wheat flour
½ cup	(125 ml)	prepared granola — any kind (plus a little extra for sprinkling on top)
1 tsp.	(5 ml)	baking powder
½ tsp.	(2 ml)	baking soda
½ tsp.	(2 ml)	cinnamon
Pinch		salt
½ cup	(125 ml)	buttermilk, thinned yogurt or sour milk (page 26)
¼ cup	(60 ml)	vegetable oil
¼ cup	(60 ml)	brown sugar
1		egg
1		medium apple, peeled and chopped

Preheat the oven to 400°F (200°C). Grease a 12-cup muffin pan or line with paper liners.

In a medium bowl, stir together the all-purpose flour, whole wheat flour, granola, baking powder, baking soda, cinnamon and salt.

In another bowl, whisk together the buttermilk (or other liquid), oil, sugar and egg until well blended. Add the flour mixture to the egg mixture and stir to combine. Fold in the chopped apple — mix well. Spoon the batter into 8 to 10 of the compartments in the prepared muffin pan, filling the cups almost to the top. Sprinkle the top of each unbaked muffin with a little bit of granola. Bake for 20 to 25 minutes, or until a toothpick poked into the middle of a muffin comes out clean.

Makes 8 to 10 muffins.

Raggedy-Ass Breakfast Muffins

Sure, these muffins really do look like they've just gotten out of bed. But they're delicious, nutritious and have plenty of spunk — the perfect muffin to kick-start your day.

1 cup	(250 ml)	rolled oats — quick cooking or old-fashioned (not instant)
¾ cup	(175 ml)	all-purpose flour
½ cup	(125 ml)	whole wheat flour
½ cup	(125 ml)	brown sugar
2 tsp.	(10 ml)	baking powder
½ tsp.	(2 ml)	baking soda
⅓ cup	(75 ml)	milk
¼ cup	(60 ml)	vegetable oil
1 tsp.	(5 ml)	vanilla extract
1		banana, mashed
1½ cups	(375 ml)	shredded carrot (about 2 medium carrots)
½ cup	(125 ml)	raisins or dried cranberries

Preheat the oven to 400°F (200°C). Grease a 12-cup muffin pan or line with paper liners.

In a large bowl, stir together the oats, all-purpose flour, whole wheat flour, brown sugar, baking powder and baking soda. In a medium bowl, whisk together the milk, oil, vanilla and banana. Add the banana mixture to the flour mixture and stir just until combined, then add the shredded carrots and raisins, and mix well, making sure that there are no pockets of unmixed flour. The batter will be very lumpy. Spoon batter into prepared muffin pan, filling the cups almost to the top. Bake for 20 to 25 minutes, or until muffins are lightly browned on top and a toothpick poked into the middle of a muffin comes out clean.

Makes about 12 muffins.

Cappuccino Chip Muffins

You're sitting at a café, reading a book by an obscure nineteenth-century French philosopher. You're drinking espresso. And eating a muffin. Not just any muffin. This muffin. You don't need to explain anything.

2 cups	(500 ml)	all-purpose flour
½ cup	(125 ml)	granulated sugar
1 tbsp.	(15 ml)	baking powder
1 tbsp.	(15 ml)	instant coffee powder
½ tsp.	(2 ml)	cinnamon
1 cup	(250 ml)	milk
1		egg
½ cup	(125 ml)	vegetable oil
½ cup	(125 ml)	semisweet chocolate chips

Preheat the oven to 375°F (190°C). Grease a 12-cup muffin pan or line with paper liners.

In a large bowl, stir together the flour, sugar, baking powder, instant coffee and cinnamon. (If your instant coffee is in big chunky crystals, crush it into a powder before adding so that it mixes more evenly.)

In another bowl, beat together the milk, egg and vegetable oil. Add to the flour mixture and stir just until combined. Mix in the chocolate chips. Don't overbeat — just mix everything and leave it alone.

Spoon batter into the prepared muffin pan, filling the cups about ¾ full. Bake for 18 to 20 minutes, or until muffins pass the toothpick test (page 23). Remove from the pan and let cool slightly before serving. If you can stand to wait that long.

Makes 8 to 10 muffins.

Whole Wheat Positive

You can substitute whole wheat flour for all or part of the all-purpose flour in this recipe. Start with a small proportion, and if you like the result, you can use more whole wheat flour next time.

Chocolate Chocolate Muffins

Chocolate Chocolate Chocolate Muffins

Want to be really bad? Are you sure? Okay, then — drizzle the muffins with Chocolate Ganache Glaze (page 171). There. Now you've done it.

Okay, here's where we draw the line. These muffins are absolutely not a healthy breakfast item. They are not low fat. Or low cholesterol. Or low anything. For your own safety, please consume responsibly.

2 cups	(500 ml)	all-purpose flour
1 cup	(250 ml)	granulated sugar
1 tsp.	(5 ml)	baking soda
½ cup	(125 ml)	butter
3 squares		(1 oz./28 g each) unsweetened chocolate
1 cup	(250 ml)	buttermilk, thinned yogurt or sour milk (see page 26)
1		egg
2 tsp.	(10 ml)	vanilla
1 cup	(250 ml)	semisweet chocolate chips

Preheat the oven to 400°F (200°C). Grease a 12-cup muffin pan or line with paper liners.

In a medium bowl, stir together the flour, sugar and baking soda. Set aside.

In a medium saucepan over low heat, melt together the butter and the unsweetened chocolate. Stir until smooth, then remove from heat and let cool until just warm to the touch. Add the buttermilk (or other liquid), egg and vanilla, and whisk the mixture until everything is well combined. Stir in the flour mixture, mixing just until all the ingredients are moistened. Add the chocolate chips and mix until the chips are evenly distributed. Then stop.

Spoon batter into the prepared muffin pan, filling the cups to the top. Bake for 15 to 20 minutes, until a toothpick poked into the middle of a muffin comes out clean. Let cool for a couple of minutes before trying to remove from the pan. Then let cool on a rack more or less completely.

Yikes. Makes about 10 Chocolate Chocolate Muffins.

Whole Wheat Positive
You can substitute whole wheat flour for all or part of the all-purpose flour in this recipe. Start with a small proportion, and if you like the result, you can use more whole wheat flour next time.

Biscuits

Go-with-Anything Biscuits

These biscuits are just as good with butter and jam for breakfast as they are plunked on top of a stew for supper.

2 cups	(500 ml)	all-purpose flour
1 tbsp.	(15 ml)	baking powder
1 tsp.	(5 ml)	granulated sugar
½ tsp.	(2 ml)	salt
⅓ cup	(75 ml)	cold butter, cut into chunks
¾ cup	(175 ml)	milk

Preheat the oven to 450°F (230°C). Have ready a cookie sheet, but don't grease it.

In a mixing bowl, or in the bowl of a food processor, mix the flour, baking powder, sugar and salt. Add the butter to the flour mixture, cutting it in with a pastry blender (or, if using a processor, with quick on-off pulses) until the mixture resembles coarse cornmeal. If you used a processor, transfer the mixture to a bowl. All at once, stir in the milk by hand, and mix until it forms a soft dough. Dump onto a lightly floured surface and lightly knead 10 or 12 times, just until it's pliable. The dough should just barely hold together.

With a rolling pin, gently roll or pat the dough out until it's about ½ inch (1 cm) thick. Cut with a round cookie cutter (2 inches/5 cm is a good size) and arrange on the prepared cookie sheet. Re-form the scraps and continue cutting until you've used all the dough. Bake for 12 to 14 minutes, until lightly browned on top and nicely puffed.

Serve warm. With anything.

Makes 8 to 10 biscuits.

Whole Wheat Positive
You can substitute whole wheat flour for all or part of the all-purpose flour in this recipe. Start with a small proportion, and if you like the result, you can use more whole wheat flour next time.

Go-with-Anything Buttermilk Biscuits

The tangy flavor of buttermilk gives homemade biscuits a little extra something or other. So if you have buttermilk in the house, try this: Reduce the baking powder to 2 tsp. (10 ml) and add ¼ tsp. (1 ml) baking soda to the dry mixture. Substitute buttermilk for the regular milk. Otherwise, mix and bake as usual.

What was that about a stew?

Okay, so let's say you've made a pot of stew. Transfer the fully cooked stew to an ovenproof casserole dish and arrange unbaked biscuits over the top (they don't have to touch — they'll expand in the oven). Bake at 400°F (200°C) for 20 to 25 minutes, or until the stew is bubbling and the biscuits are lightly browned.

Fruit Yogurt Scones

How to Measure Butter Without Using Bad Words

Measuring solid butter is a messy, annoying business that can make you all aggravated. Packing the butter solidly into the measuring cup to get exactly the right amount is awkward, and then it sticks to the cup when you try to get it out. What you need is a shortcut.

Let's say the recipe calls for ½ cup (125 ml) butter. Fill a measuring cup with cold (!) water to the ½ cup (125 ml) level, then add chunks of butter to the measuring cup until the water reaches the 1 cup (250 ml) level. Pour off all the water, and ta-da! You have ½ cup (125 ml) of butter.

This method works just as well with any solid fat such as margarine, lard or vegetable shortening.

Lovely with a pot of Earl Grey tea, creamy butter and strawberry jam.

2½ cups	(600 ml)	all-purpose flour
1 tbsp.	(15 ml)	baking powder
¼ cup	(60 ml)	granulated sugar
½ cup	(125 ml)	cold butter, cut into chunks
¾ cup	(175 ml)	fruit yogurt, any flavor

Preheat the oven to 425°F (220°C). Have ready a cookie sheet, but don't grease it.

Stir together the flour, baking powder and sugar in a large bowl. Add the butter chunks and, using a pastry blender or two knives, cut the butter into the flour mixture until it looks like coarse oatmeal. (See cutting in shortening — page 179.)

Add the yogurt to the crumbly mixture and stir just until it forms a soft dough that can be pressed together into a ball. Dump the dough onto a lightly floured surface and knead 4 or 5 times, just until it's smooth. Please resist the temptation to overwork the dough. Excessive kneading will make it tough.

Divide the dough in half. Sprinkle your counter or other work surface with flour. Working with one half at a time, gently pat or roll the dough down on the floured surface into a 4-inch (10 cm) circle, about ½ inch (1 cm) thick. With a sharp knife, cut into 6 wedges (for that traditional scone look). Repeat with the remaining dough. Place scones on the prepared cookie sheet, slightly apart (to allow for rising), and bake for 12 to 14 minutes, until lightly browned.

Makes 12 very dainty scones.

Whole Wheat Positive

You can substitute whole wheat flour for all or part of the all-purpose flour in this recipe. Start with a small proportion, and if you like the result, you can use more whole wheat flour next time.

Cheddar Biscuits

These are great with a bowl of soup, but there's no law against serving them with scrambled eggs or using them to make little appetizer sandwiches to serve with good mustard and thinly sliced ham.

2 cups	(500 ml)	all-purpose flour
1 tbsp.	(15 ml)	baking powder
1 tbsp.	(15 ml)	granulated sugar
½ tsp.	(2 ml)	salt
¼ cup	(60 ml)	butter
1¼ cups	(300 ml)	shredded cheddar cheese
¾ cup	(175 ml)	milk

Preheat the oven to 450°F (230°C). Have ready a cookie sheet, but don't grease it.

In a large bowl, or in the bowl of a food processor, mix the flour, baking powder, sugar and salt. Cut in the butter with a pastry blender (or by processing in short on-off pulses) until the mixture looks like coarse oatmeal. If using a processor, transfer to a bowl. Stir in the shredded cheese and toss to combine. Add the milk all at once, and stir until it forms a soft dough. Dump onto a lightly floured surface and knead lightly by hand 10 or 12 times, until smooth.

With a rolling pin, roll out the dough to a thickness of ½ inch (1 cm). Cut into rounds — 2 inches (5 cm) in diameter is a good size — and place on the prepared cookie sheet. Bake for 12 to 14 minutes, until the biscuits are lightly browned and nicely puffed.

Makes 8 to 10 biscuits.

Whole Wheat Positive
You can substitute whole wheat flour for all or part of the all-purpose flour in this recipe. Start with a small proportion, and if you like the result, you can use more whole wheat flour next time.

Choose Your Cheese

No cheddar in your refrigerator? No problem. Use whatever cheese you happen to have — even a mixture of shriveled odds and ends. Swiss, Monterey Jack, havarti, provolone, even blue cheese. Very interesting.

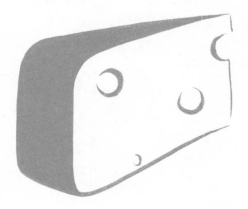

Olive Oil Scones with Herbs and Garlic

Handy Herbs

Use whichever dried herbs you like to make these scones. You can buy a ready-made blend (like Italian blend or Herbes de Provence) or mix up your own. Even better — if you happen to have some fresh herbs available, use up to 2 tbsp. (30 ml) chopped fresh rosemary, thyme, oregano or basil instead of the dried.

These make a delicious appetizer with a wedge of cheese and a few olives. Or serve the scones with a bowl of soup. Impossibly easy.

2 cups	(500 ml)	all-purpose flour
¼ cup	(60 ml)	grated Parmesan cheese
1 tbsp.	(15 ml)	baking powder
½ tsp.	(2 ml)	salt
¼ tsp.	(1 ml)	black pepper
½ cup	(125 ml)	plain yogurt
⅓ cup	(75 ml)	olive oil
1		egg
1		clove garlic, minced
1 tbsp.	(15 ml)	crumbled dried oregano, basil, thyme, rosemary (or a mixture)

Preheat the oven to 375°F (190°C). Lightly grease a cookie sheet.

In a large bowl, mix the flour, Parmesan cheese, baking powder, salt and pepper.

In another bowl, whisk together the yogurt, oil, egg, garlic and dried herbs until it forms a gloppy mixture. Add the yogurt mixture to the flour mixture, stirring until it becomes a soft dough. Dump the dough onto a lightly floured surface and knead for 10 or 12 strokes, until the dough is smooth and pliable. Divide into two lumps.

With a rolling pin, roll out one lump of dough to a 5-inch (13 cm) circle. With a sharp knife, cut it pizzawise into 8 wedges. Arrange the wedges on the prepared cookie sheet. Repeat with the second half of the dough. Bake for 15 to 20 minutes, until lightly browned on top. Serve immediately (they're not nearly as good cold).

Makes 16 scones.

Whole Wheat Positive

You can substitute whole wheat flour for all or part of the all-purpose flour in this recipe. Start with a small proportion, and if you like the result, you can use more whole wheat flour next time.

Homemade Biscuit Mix

What we have here is a kinder, gentler version of that pantry staple: commercial biscuit mix. This mix, made with real butter and no weird ingredients whatsoever, can be used in any recipe that calls for the store-bought kind, but you'll feel better about it because you made it yourself. It will keep, refrigerated, for a long time.

9 cups	(2.25 liters)	all-purpose flour (or a mixture of all-purpose and whole wheat flours)
¼ cup	(60 ml)	baking powder
2 tsp.	(10 ml)	salt
2 tsp.	(10 ml)	cream of tartar
1 tsp.	(5 ml)	baking soda
1 lb.	(454 g)	cold butter

In a large bowl, stir together the flour, baking powder, salt, cream of tartar and baking soda until well mixed.

Using a pastry blender, cut the butter into the flour mixture until the mixture resembles coarse cornmeal. This can also be done in 2 or 3 batches in a food processor — just make sure you divide the ingredients equally and don't overprocess the mixture. It should remain mealy.

Store the mix in the refrigerator or freezer in a tightly covered container. Use in any recipe that calls for commercial biscuit mix.

Makes about 10 cups (2.5 liters).

Making Biscuits Using Homemade Mix

Nothing could be easier. Except not making biscuits at all. But what fun is that?
Preheat the oven to 425°F (220°C). Have ready a cookie sheet, but don't grease it.

Stir 2 cups (500 ml) of Homemade Biscuit Mix together with ½ cup (125 ml) milk just until a soft dough forms.

Gently roll or pat the dough out on a lightly floured surface to a thickness of about ½ inch (1 cm). Cut biscuits out with a 2-inch (5 cm) round cutter and place on the prepared cookie sheet. Place in the oven and bake for 10 to 12 minutes, until lightly browned.

Done.

Makes 10 to 12 biscuits.

Quick Little Dinner Buns

Not a muffin, but not exactly a regular dinner roll either. These buns are really too easy to be so good. Great with a bowl of soup or chili.

2 cups	**(500 ml)**	**all-purpose flour**
2 tsp.	**(10 ml)**	**baking powder**
½ tsp.	**(2 ml)**	**salt**
1½ cups	**(375 ml)**	**milk**
6 tbsp.	**(90 ml)**	**mayonnaise**

Preheat the oven to 400°F (200°C). Grease a 12-cup muffin pan.

In a mixing bowl, stir together the flour, baking powder and salt. Add the milk and mayonnaise, and stir with a fork until everything is blended and the mixture is smooth. Spoon into the prepared muffin pan, filling the cups about ⅔ full. Bake for 20 to 25 minutes, until the tops are lightly browned.

Remove from pan and let cool for just a few minutes before serving.

Makes 8 to 10 quick little buns.

Whole Wheat Positive
You can substitute whole wheat flour for all or part of the all-purpose flour in this recipe. Start with a small proportion, and if you like the result, you can use more whole wheat flour next time.

Clueless Troubleshooting: Muffins and Biscuits

Muffins and biscuits should be simple and straightforward and give you no trouble at all. But sometimes they misbehave. Here's some help in tracking down the problem so that next time you can show them who's boss.

They didn't rise at all.

✓ Did you add the baking powder or baking soda? Are you sure you added it?

✓ How old is your baking powder/soda? Older than your car? Buy a fresh package — it doesn't last forever.

✓ Did the batter hang around too long before baking? While it is sometimes okay to let the batter sit for a while before baking, not all recipes can handle the wait. If your recipe says to put it in the oven immediately — do it.

They rose nicely, then collapsed.

✓ Did you take them out of the oven before they were fully baked? Do the toothpick test next time (see page 23).

✓ Don't open the oven door every two minutes to see how they're doing. Fluctuating oven temperature can cause muffins to collapse.

The bottoms burned before the muffins or biscuits were fully baked.

✓ Try moving your pan to a higher shelf next time. Or simply lower the heat by 10 to 25 degrees. Your oven may heat unevenly.

✓ Get an oven thermometer and use it to make sure your oven is actually running at the right temperature.

My muffins are pointy! What's up with that?

✓ The batter was overbeaten. Didn't I tell you not to do that?

All the blueberries sank to the bottom of the muffins.

✓ Toss the blueberries with a little of the flour from the recipe before adding them to the batter. Sometimes this helps suspend the berries. (Sometimes it doesn't.)

My muffins refuse to come out of the pan.

✓ Invest in a nonstick muffin pan.
✓ Grease the cups with vegetable oil cooking spray.
✓ If all else fails, use paper liners.

The muffins look fine, but they taste, uh, funny.

✓ The dry ingredients may not have been evenly mixed. Lumps of baking soda or baking powder can give baked goods an icky flavor. Make sure you mix (or even sift) dry ingredients together before adding the liquids.
✓ Were your ingredients fresh? Really now — were they? Nothing can disguise the taste of stale nuts, rancid oil or funky whole wheat flour. Throw the muffins away. Or feed them to the birds. Treat yourself to fresh ingredients and keep them refrigerated.

Cookies, Cookies and More Cookies

Cookies

You don't need a reason to bake cookies. Cookies exist in a universe all their own — pointless, but wonderful. A tiny bit of something delicious, that can be eaten without a fork or plate. Cookies can be tossed into a brown paper lunch bag, piled in an old wicker basket or arranged tastefully on an antique silver platter. It makes no difference — a good cookie will always be an excellent thing.

Crisp Oatmeal Cookies

This is a classic oatmeal cookie — crisp enough to improve by dunking in a glass of chocolate milk.

½ cup	(125 ml)	butter
½ cup	(125 ml)	granulated sugar
½ cup	(125 ml)	brown sugar
1		egg
1 tsp.	(5 ml)	vanilla extract
1 cup	(250 ml)	all-purpose or whole wheat flour (or a mixture)
½ tsp.	(2 ml)	baking powder
½ tsp.	(2 ml)	baking soda
½ cup	(125 ml)	quick-cooking rolled oats (not instant)
1 cup	(250 ml)	unsweetened shredded coconut

Preheat the oven to 375°F (190°C). Line one or two cookie sheets with parchment paper.

In a large mixing bowl, beat together the butter, granulated sugar, brown sugar, egg and vanilla with an electric mixer, until blended and creamy.

Add the flour, baking powder and baking soda, and beat until mixed. Stir in the oats and coconut — mix well.

Drop dough by teaspoonfuls onto the prepared cookie sheet, leaving 2 inches (5 cm) between them to allow for spreading. Bake for 9 to 12 minutes, until lightly browned around the edges.

Makes about 3 dozen cookies.

Baker's Parchment Paper

Baker's parchment is a heavy, nonstick paper, specifically intended for cooking and baking. If you don't already have a roll of the stuff in your cupboard, you should run out right now and buy some. It's much better than waxed paper for lining the bottom of cake pans (so that your cakes don't stick) and is an absolute miracle for baking cookies. A cookie sheet lined with baking parchment can be reused several times before the paper has to be replaced, and will leave you with a perfectly clean baking sheet after you're all done. The nonstick surface may also allow you get away with just lightly greasing the pan, or eliminate the need for greasing altogether.

You can use parchment paper for other cooking purposes as well — such as cooking fish or chicken in fancy little packets or covering a casserole to retain moisture.

And in a pinch, your kids can trace a map of South America on it for that geography project that's supposed to be handed in by Wednesday.

Tips for the Cookie-Baking Perfectionist

✓ Drop cookies have the irritating tendency to be unevenly shaped, odd sizes and annoyingly imperfect. If this bothers you, chill the dough for several hours before baking to firm it up. You can then roll it by hand into identical, perfect balls and place them in precise geometric rows on your cookie sheet for baking.

✓ Use a miniature ice cream scoop to accurately measure out your cookie dough onto the baking sheet. *Heaping teaspoon* is such a vague term, isn't it?

✓ When making slice-and-bake cookies, freeze the logs of dough before slicing so that the cylinders don't get squashed when you're cutting them. There — perfectly round cookies.

✓ When rolling out cookie dough, place two chopsticks (or some other stick of the proper thickness) on the counter to use as a guide for your rolling pin. That way, all your cookies will be the exactly the same thickness.

Big Chewy Oatmeal Raisin Cookies

Help! My brown sugar is hard as a rock!

Don't panic. Just put a chunk of fresh apple into a jar or other airtight container with the hard sugar and go away for 24 hours. When you come back, the apple will look as if it's had a rough night, but your brown sugar will be perfectly soft and ready to use.

If this is an emergency, measure the amount of brown sugar you need for your recipe into a microwave-safe bowl. Nuke on high power for short, 30-second bursts, until the sugar is softened. Use immediately — it will resolidify when it cools.

Whole Wheat Positive
You can substitute whole wheat flour for all or part of the all-purpose flour in this recipe. Start with a small proportion, and if you like the result, you can use more whole wheat flour next time.

To appreciate the full effect of these wonderfully satisfying cookies, you really should have a nice, cold glass of milk on the side. It's just the right thing to do.

1 cup	(250 ml)	raisins, divided
⅓ cup	(75 ml)	water
1½ cups	(375 ml)	brown sugar
½ cup	(125 ml)	butter
1		egg
2 tsp.	(10 ml)	vanilla extract
2 cups	(500 ml)	all-purpose flour
1¼ cups	(300 ml)	rolled oats (old-fashioned or quick, not instant)
1 tsp.	(5 ml)	baking soda
½ tsp.	(2 ml)	cinnamon
¼ tsp.	(1 ml)	salt

Preheat the oven to 350°F (180°C). Line one or two cookie sheets with parchment paper.

In a blender or food processor, combine ½ cup (125 ml) of the raisins (pay attention — this is only half of them!) with the water and blend until it forms a gloppy brown puree. Reserve the remaining raisins — you'll need them later.

In a large mixing bowl, with an electric mixer, beat together the raisin puree, brown sugar, butter, egg and vanilla until smooth.

In another bowl, stir together the flour, oats, baking soda, cinnamon and salt. Combine this mixture with the egg mixture and beat until all the ingredients are evenly mixed. Stir in the reserved raisins (remember them?).

By hand, roll the dough into golf-ball-size balls and arrange them on the prepared cookie sheets about 2 inches (5 cm) apart to allow them to spread. Bake for 12 to 15 minutes, until lightly browned on the bottom. Remove to a rack and let cool.

Makes 2 to 3 dozen big, chewy cookies.

Whole Wheat Peanut Butter Banana Lumps

The classic lunchbox sandwich reimagined as a soft, cakey cookie. Brilliant.

2 cups	(500 ml)	whole wheat flour
2 tsp.	(10 ml)	baking powder
1 cup	(250 ml)	brown sugar
¾ cup	(175 ml)	peanut butter
¼ cup	(60 ml)	butter
2		ripe bananas, peeled and cut into chunks
2		eggs

Preheat the oven to 350°F (180°C). Line one or two cookie sheets with parchment paper and grease the paper lightly.

In a large bowl, stir together the all-purpose flour, whole wheat flour and baking powder. Set aside.

Into the container of a blender or food processor, place the brown sugar, peanut butter, butter, bananas and eggs. Whirl until smooth, scraping down the sides once or twice. Pour the banana mixture into the flour mixture, and stir until evenly combined into a thick batter.

Drop dough by heaping teaspoonfuls onto the prepared cookie sheets, leaving enough room between the cookies for expansion. Bake for 13 to 15 minutes, until cookies are set and lightly browned on the bottom.

Makes 4 dozen lumpy cookies.

Gluten-Free Friendly
Substitute gluten-free all-purpose flour for the regular all-purpose flour in this recipe. Results may differ slightly from the original version.

Variation

Chocolate chips? Why not?

Add ½ cup (125 ml) semisweet chocolate chips to the batter. Go ahead. Do it.

Killer Chocolate Chip Cookies

Dangerously overloaded with chocolate chips, these cookies are definitely worth the risk. Some say they're the best ever. You be the judge of that.

1 cup	(250 ml)	butter
½ cup	(125 ml)	granulated sugar
1½ cups	(375 ml)	brown sugar
2		eggs
2½ tsp.	(12 ml)	vanilla extract
2½ cups	(625 ml)	all-purpose flour
½ tsp.	(2 ml)	salt
1 tsp.	(5 ml)	baking powder
1 tsp.	(5 ml)	baking soda
2½ cups	(625 ml)	semisweet chocolate chips

Preheat the oven to 350°F (180°C). Line one or two cookie sheets with parchment paper.

In a large mixing bowl, with an electric mixer, beat together the butter, granulated sugar, brown sugar, eggs and vanilla, beating until smooth and creamy.

In another bowl, stir together the flour, salt, baking powder and baking soda. Add the flour mixture to the butter mixture, beating until everything is evenly combined. Stir in the chocolate chips.

By hand, form the dough into golf-ball-size balls and place them 2 inches (5 cm) apart on the prepared cookie sheets. Bake for 9 to 10 minutes, just until the edges are beginning to brown lightly. These cookies are best when they're slightly underbaked, so remove them from the oven while they're still a bit soft in the middle, and let cool on a rack.

Makes 2 to 3 dozen chocolate chip cookies of your dreams.

Whole Wheat Positive
You can substitute whole wheat flour for all or part of the all-purpose flour in this recipe. Start with a small proportion, and if you like the result, you can use more whole wheat flour next time.

Giant Snickerdoodles

Is it an extinct flightless bird? A Sesame Street character? A Victorian undergarment? None of the above. It's just a great big cookie — perfect for dunking into your latte.

1½ cups	(375 ml)	granulated sugar
1 cup	(250 ml)	butter
2		eggs
2¾ cups	(650 ml)	all-purpose flour
2 tsp.	(10 ml)	cream of tartar
1 tsp.	(5 ml)	baking soda

Cinnamon sugar coating

1 tbsp.	(15 ml)	cinnamon
3 tbsp.	(45 ml)	granulated sugar

In a large bowl, with an electric mixer, beat together the 1½ cups (375 ml) sugar, butter and eggs until light and fluffy — about 5 minutes. Scrape down the sides a few times to keep things well mixed.

In another bowl, stir together the flour, cream of tartar and baking soda. Add to the butter mixture, beating until well blended. Refrigerate dough for at least half an hour (or longer) to allow it to firm up so that you can handle it.

Preheat the oven to 375°F (190°C). Line one or two cookies sheets with parchment paper.

In flat bowl or pie plate, stir together the ingredients for the cinnamon sugar coating. By hand, shape the dough into 2-inch (5 cm) balls (remember, these are *giant* snickerdoodles) and roll each one in the cinnamon sugar until it is coated all over. Place on the prepared baking sheets, at least 3 inches (8 cm) apart — they will spread a lot. Bake for 12 to 15 minutes, until cookies are firm around the edges — the middle will still be a bit soft. Remove to a rack to cool.

Makes about 2½ dozen giant flightless cookies.

Whole Wheat Positive
You can substitute whole wheat flour for all or part of the all-purpose flour in this recipe. Start with a small proportion, and if you like the result, you can use more whole wheat flour next time.

Regular Everyday Peanut Butter Cookies

You simply can't argue with a peanut butter cookie. It's a lunchbox classic.

½ cup	(125 ml)	butter
½ cup	(125 ml)	creamy peanut butter
½ cup	(125 ml)	granulated sugar
½ cup	(125 ml)	brown sugar
1		egg
1¼ cups	(300 ml)	all-purpose or whole wheat flour (or a mixture)
½ tsp.	(2 ml)	baking powder
½ tsp.	(2 ml)	baking soda

Preheat the oven to 375°F (190°C). Line one or two cookie sheets with parchment paper.

In a large mixing bowl, with an electric mixer, beat together the butter, peanut butter, white sugar, brown sugar and egg until creamy and thoroughly mixed. Add the flour, baking powder and baking soda, and blend very well. That's it for the dough.

Now make the cookies: by hand, roll the dough into 1-inch (2 cm) balls, then arrange them on the prepared cookie sheets, leaving 2 inches (5 cm) between them to allow for spreading. For the classic peanut butter cookie look, flatten each ball of dough with the tines of a fork, pressing lightly to make a crisscross pattern. There — isn't that just lovely? Bake for 10 to 12 minutes, until the cookies have puffed slightly and are lightly browned on the bottom.

Makes about 3½ dozen.

Flourless Peanut Butter Cookies

*A perfect, gluten-free alternative to the classic. So good and so easy —
quite amazing, really.*

1 cup	**(250 ml)**	**smooth peanut butter**
1 cup	**(250 ml)**	**granulated sugar**
1		**egg**
1 tsp.	**(5 ml)**	**vanilla extract**

Preheat the oven to 350°F (180°C). Line one or two cookie sheets
with parchment paper.

In a medium bowl, beat together the peanut butter, sugar, egg
and vanilla with an electric mixer until a smooth dough forms. By
hand, roll the dough into 1-inch (2 cm) balls and place them on the
prepared cookie sheets, at least 1½ inches (4 cm) apart. Flatten each
ball of dough with the tines of a fork, pressing lightly to make the
traditional crisscross pattern. Place in the oven and bake for 10 to 12
minutes, until cookies are golden around the edges. Remove cookies
to a wire rack to cool.

Makes about 2 dozen excellent cookies.

Deep Dark Flourless Fudge Cookies

Don't be afraid of the dark. Dark chocolate, that is. These cookies are easy, ultra-intense and totally gluten-free. The perfect thing for a chocolate fanatic.

2¼ cups	**(530 ml)**	**icing sugar**
1 cup	**(250 ml)**	**unsweetened cocoa powder**
3		**egg whites**
2 tsp.	**(10 ml)**	**vanilla extract**

Preheat the oven to 350°F (180°C). Line two cookie sheets with parchment paper and grease the paper.

In a large bowl, beat together the icing sugar, cocoa powder, egg whites and vanilla with an electric mixer just until the mixture is smooth and begins to thicken slightly. This shouldn't take more than one or two minutes.

Drop the batter by heaping teaspoonfuls onto the prepared cookie sheets, leaving at least 1½ inches (4 cm) between them — they will spread. Bake for 8 to 10 minutes, or until the cookies have puffed, but are still soft in the middle. Let cookies cool on the cookie sheets before removing.

Makes about 2 dozen deep dark cookies.

How to Separate an Egg Properly and, More Important, Why You'd Want To

For egg whites to beat properly into a fluffy, stiff foam, there cannot be a smidgen — not an iota, not a subatomic particle — of egg yolk mixed in. So learning to separate the two parts of the egg efficiently and without drama is an important baking skill. Practice your technique at a noncrucial moment ahead of time — like when you're making scrambled eggs or something and not when you're about to make your first angel food cake.

Here's how to do it. Have three bowls ready: two large ones and a small one (like a custard cup). Crack the eggshell by tapping it firmly against the side of one of the bowls. Using both hands, carefully pry the two halves apart and, holding the yolk back, let the white part drain into the *small bowl*. Gently transfer the yolk back and forth between the two half shells, letting as much of the white drip into the *small bowl* as possible. Now dump the yolk into *one of the large bowls*. Transfer the separated white from the *small bowl* to the *second large bowl*. Repeat the process with the remaining eggs.

The seemingly pointless step of separating each egg individually into a small bowl is to prevent ruining all the eggs if you happen to break the yolk on the last egg you crack. If you crack and separate them individually, you've only messed up one egg (rather than four or six). You can set the messed-up egg aside and use it for a purpose that requires a whole egg.

Hermit Cookies

You don't have to be a cave-dwelling hermit to appreciate these cookies. They're also good to share with friends. In your kitchen.

½ cup	(125 ml)	butter
1 cup	(250 ml)	brown sugar
1		egg
2 tbsp.	(30 ml)	milk
1½ cups	(375 ml)	all-purpose flour
1 tbsp.	(15 ml)	instant coffee powder
½ tsp.	(2 ml)	baking soda
½ tsp.	(2 ml)	cinnamon
¼ tsp.	(1 ml)	nutmeg
¼ tsp.	(1 ml)	cloves
¾ cup	(175 ml)	raisins
½ cup	(125 ml)	chopped walnuts

Preheat the oven to 375°F (190°C). Line one or two cookie sheets with parchment paper.

In a large mixing bowl, with an electric mixer, beat together the butter and brown sugar until just creamy. Add the egg and milk, and continue beating until smooth.

In another bowl, stir together the flour, instant coffee (if the granules are large, crush them to a powder before using), baking soda, cinnamon, nutmeg and cloves. Add the flour mixture to the butter mixture and beat just until smooth. Stir in the raisins and walnuts, and mix well.

Drop batter by heaping teaspoonfuls onto the prepared cookie sheets, about 2 inches (5 cm) apart — cookies will spread. Bake for 10 to 12 minutes, until the cookies are set and lightly browned. Remove to a rack to cool.

Makes about 2½ dozen.

Whole Wheat Positive
You can substitute whole wheat flour for all or part of the all-purpose flour in this recipe. Start with a small proportion, and if you like the result, you can use more whole wheat flour next time.

Gluten-Free Friendly
Substitute gluten-free all-purpose flour for the regular all-purpose flour in this recipe. Results may differ slightly from the original version.

Almond or Coconut Macaroons

Chewy, nutty and totally gluten-free. Not to mention easy as pie. Easier, actually.

3		egg whites
½ tsp.	(2 ml)	vanilla extract
1½ cups	(375 ml)	icing sugar
2½ cups	(600 ml)	unsweetened shredded coconut or ground almonds

Preheat the oven to 350°F (180°C). Line one or two cookie sheets with parchment paper and lightly grease the paper.

In a large bowl, beat the egg whites with an electric mixer on high speed until stiff but still glossy. Stir in the vanilla. With a rubber spatula, fold in the icing sugar and coconut or almonds, mixing just until everything is evenly mixed— don't overstir or you'll deflate the egg whites.

Drop the batter by heaping teaspoonfuls onto the prepared cookie sheets, leaving at least 1½ inches (4 cm) between them (they will puff and spread). Bake for 13 to 15 minutes, until the tops of the macaroons are lightly browned and crisp. Let cool for a few minutes before removing to a rack to cool completely.

Makes about 3 dozen.

Soft Ginger Cookies

These ginger cookies are so addictively chewy and gingery that you can easily eat a dozen of them before you even notice. Maybe that's not such a good thing.

1 cup	(250 ml)	granulated sugar
¾ cup	(175 ml)	butter
1		egg
¾ cup	(60 ml)	molasses
1 tbsp.	(15 ml)	water
2¼ cups	(550 ml)	all-purpose flour
2 tsp.	(10 ml)	ground ginger
1 tsp.	(5 ml)	baking soda
1 tsp.	(5 ml)	cinnamon
		additional granulated sugar for rolling cookies

In a large bowl, with an electric mixer, beat together the sugar and butter until creamy. Add the egg, molasses and water, and continue beating until smooth.

In another bowl, stir together the flour, ginger, baking soda and cinnamon. Add this mixture to the butter mixture, and beat until everything is thoroughly combined and a soft dough forms. Cover the bowl with plastic wrap and refrigerate for at least 30 minutes, until the dough is firm enough to handle.

Preheat the oven to 350°F (180°C). Line one or two cookie sheets with parchment paper.

Dump some sugar onto a plate. By hand, roll the dough into 1 to 1½ inch (2.5 to 4 cm) balls, then roll each ball of dough in the sugar, turning to coat all sides. Place balls on the prepared cookie sheet, about 2 inches (5 cm) apart to allow for spreading (they really will spread). Bake for 8 to 10 minutes. Now, here's the thing: these cookies will be really soft and you won't think they're ready, but take them out of the oven anyway. Let them cool for a couple of minutes on the cookie sheet, then remove them to a rack to cool completely. They will firm up. No, really they will.

Makes 3½ to 4 dozen perfect, chewy ginger cookies.

Whole Wheat Positive
You can substitute whole wheat flour for all or part of the all-purpose flour in this recipe. Start with a small proportion, and if you like the result, you can use more whole wheat flour next time.

Chocolate Crinkles

These cookies look like the aftermath of a horrible natural disaster. A drought. An earthquake. Too depressing. Don't think about it. Have a cookie.

½ cup	(125 ml)	vegetable oil
4 squares		(1 oz./28 g each) unsweetened chocolate
2 cups	(500 ml)	granulated sugar
4		eggs
2 tsp.	(10 ml)	vanilla extract
2 cups	(500 ml)	all-purpose flour
2 tsp.	(10 ml)	baking powder
1 cup	(250 ml)	icing sugar

Chocolate Sparkle Variation

Roll the balls of dough in granulated sugar instead of icing sugar for a sparkly, if somewhat less apocalyptic-looking, cookie.

In a small saucepan, combine the oil and the chocolate and place over low heat, stirring until the chocolate is melted and the mixture is smooth. Transfer to a mixing bowl. Add the sugar, eggs and vanilla, and beat with an electric mixer until smooth and well blended. Mix in the flour and baking powder, and beat just until the flour is incorporated into the dough. Cover the bowl with plastic wrap and place in the refrigerator for at least 2 hours or overnight, until the dough is firm enough to shape by hand.

Preheat the oven to 350°F (180°C). Line one or two cookie sheets with parchment paper and grease the paper lightly.

Sprinkle the icing sugar into a flat bowl or pie plate. By hand, form the dough into 1-inch (2 cm) balls and roll each one in the icing sugar until completely coated. Place on the prepared cookie sheet, at least 1½ inches (4 cm) apart. Bake for 10 to 12 minutes, until the cookies are puffed and crackled, but still slightly soft in the center. Remove to a rack to cool.

Makes 5½ to 6 dozen dramatically crinkled cookies.

Whole Wheat Positive
You can substitute whole wheat flour for all or part of the all-purpose flour in this recipe. Start with a small proportion, and if you like the result, you can use more whole wheat flour next time.

Health-Nut Cookies

Packed to the rafters with all kinds of nuts and seeds and whole grains, these are seriously nutritious cookies. You can adjust the ingredients to suit your taste and your budget as long as you keep the total amount of nuts, seeds and dried fruit the same.

1½ cups	(375 ml)	raisins, currants or dried cranberries
1 cup	(250 ml)	chopped walnuts
1 cup	(250 ml)	chopped pecans
1 cup	(250 ml)	peanuts
1 cup	(250 ml)	quick-cooking rolled oats (not instant)
½ cup	(125 ml)	pine nuts
½ cup	(125 ml)	sunflower seeds
½ cup	(125 ml)	sesame seeds
½ cup	(125 ml)	wheat germ
1 cup	(250 ml)	whole wheat flour
2 tsp.	(10 ml)	baking powder
1 tsp.	(5 ml)	cinnamon
½ tsp.	(2 ml)	ground ginger
1 cup	(250 ml)	butter
½ cup	(125 ml)	peanut butter
1¼ cups	(300 ml)	brown sugar
2		eggs
¼ cup	(60 ml)	milk

Preheat the oven to 350°F (180°C). Line one or two cookie sheets with parchment paper and grease the paper lightly.

In a very large bowl, combine the raisins (or whatever), walnuts, pecans, peanuts, oats, pine nuts, sunflower seeds, sesame seeds and wheat germ. Toss until well mixed.

In a small bowl, stir together the whole wheat flour, baking powder, cinnamon and ginger. Add this mixture to the fruit-and-nut mixture, and stir until everything is combined.

In another bowl, with an electric mixer, cream together the butter, peanut butter and brown sugar until fluffy — about 5 minutes. Add the eggs and milk, and beat until thoroughly mixed. With a large spoon, mix the butter mixture into the dry ingredients, stirring until everything is evenly mushed together. The mixture should be moist enough to hold together as a thick dough.

With a ¼ cup (60 ml) measuring cup, scoop the dough onto the prepared cookie sheet, placing the scoops at least 2 inches (5 cm) apart. Bake for 16 to 18 minutes, until cookies are lightly browned on the bottom and set. They will still be a little soft on top.

Makes 3 dozen big, outrageously nutritious cookies.

Now go out hiking or something.

Flour: To Sift or Not to Sift ... That Is the Question

You're thinking, Awww — do I have to?

The answer is a definite maybe. The whole point of sifting flour is to remove lumps and to make the flour light and fluffy. When you buy a bag of flour, it has already been sifted, so you're not likely to find any lumps in it. But if it has been sitting on the shelf for a few months, it may have settled and become compressed — it's no longer as light and fluffy as it should be. So should you sift it? Sometimes.

Yes, sift.
- ✓ If you're making a cake where a light and fluffy texture is important
- ✓ If you can actually see lumps in the flour
- ✓ If you want to combine evenly: for instance, cocoa powder or spices with flour
- ✓ If you feel like it (it'll never do any harm)

No, don't bother.
- ✓ If you're baking bread
- ✓ If you're making a moist, heavy cake or muffins
- ✓ If you're making cookies

Chocolate Damnation Cookies

No. Stop. Don't make these.

10 squares		**(1 oz./28 g each) semisweet chocolate**
1 cup	**(250 ml)**	**brown sugar**
½ cup	**(125 ml)**	**granulated sugar**
½ cup	**(125 ml)**	**butter**
4		**eggs**
1 tsp.	**(5 ml)**	**vanilla extract**
2¼ cups	**(550 ml)**	**all-purpose flour**
1 tsp.	**(5 ml)**	**baking powder**
1 tsp.	**(5 ml)**	**baking soda**
1 tbsp.	**(15 ml)**	**black coffee (leftover is fine)**
2 cups	**(500 ml)**	**semisweet chocolate chips or coarsely chopped semisweet chocolate**
1 cup	**(250 ml)**	**coarsely chopped pecans**
1 cup	**(250 ml)**	**dried cranberries or dried cherries (optional but excellent)**

Place the chocolate squares in a double boiler or a saucepan set over a pan of hot (not boiling) water, and stir until the chocolate is melted and smooth. Remove from heat and let cool slightly while you prepare the remaining ingredients.

In a large mixing bowl, beat together the brown sugar, granulated sugar and butter with an electric mixer until smooth and creamy. Add the eggs and vanilla, and continue beating until well blended. Beat in the melted chocolate, then stir in the flour, baking powder, baking soda and coffee, mixing everything well. Now add the chocolate chips or chopped chocolate, the pecans, the cranberries or cherries, and stir until everything is evenly distributed. Cover the bowl with plastic wrap and chill for about an hour to allow the dough to firm up.

Preheat the oven to 350°F (180°C). Line one or two cookie sheets with parchment paper.

Place golf-ball-size (or slightly larger) balls of dough on the prepared cookie sheet, about 2 inches (5 cm) apart. Bake until just set — 13 to 15 minutes. These cookies are best if you undercook them slightly, so remove them from the oven while they're still a bit soft — they'll firm up as they cool.

Makes about 2 dozen bad, bad (but very good) cookies.

Whole Wheat Positive
You can substitute whole wheat flour for all or part of the all-purpose flour in this recipe. Start with a small proportion, and if you like the result, you can use more whole wheat flour next time.

How to Melt Chocolate

Sure, you can leave a chocolate bar in the glove compartment of your car and it will melt. But it won't melt properly. Here's how to do it right (and avoid messing up your road maps).

In a double boiler

Place as much chocolate as you'll need, broken up into chunks, into the top section of a double boiler. Fill the bottom section with hot water and place on the stove. Bring the water to a simmer over medium heat, then turn off the heat and let the chocolate melt, stirring until smooth.

Without a double boiler

Break chocolate up into chunks and place in a small saucepan. Set the small saucepan into a slightly bigger saucepan or skillet. Add hot water to the larger pan. Be careful not to let a single drop of water slosh into the chocolate (it will make the chocolate clump). Place the two pans over medium heat and bring the water to a simmer. Turn off the heat and let the chocolate melt, stirring until smooth.

In a microwave

Chop your chocolate into chunks and place in a microwave-safe bowl. Microwave on medium power, in 30-second bursts, for a total of 2 to 3 minutes (for 2 squares), stirring after each burst. Increase the amount of time (30 seconds at a time) if you're melting more than 2 squares of chocolate. Watch carefully — chocolate can scorch easily in the microwave.

Lacy Almond Crisps

These pretty cookies are really fun to watch as they bake. Just be careful not to let them burn — the baking time is very short.

6 tbsp.	(90 ml)	butter
⅓ cup	(75 ml)	brown sugar
3 tbsp.	(45 ml)	corn syrup
¾ cup	(175 ml)	finely ground almonds
⅓ cup	(75 ml)	all-purpose flour
1 tsp.	(5 ml)	vanilla extract
½ cup	(125 ml)	semisweet chocolate chips, melted (optional but excellent)

Preheat the oven to 350°F (180°C). Line one or two cookie sheets with parchment paper.

In a medium saucepan, combine butter, brown sugar and corn syrup. Bring to a boil over medium heat, stirring constantly. Remove from heat and stir in almonds, flour and vanilla. Mix well.

Drop batter by little half-teaspoonfuls, 3 inches (8 cm) apart on the prepared cookie sheet. Yes, that's just a tiny bit of dough — but trust me, it's magic. Bake for 5 to 7 minutes until the cookies turn golden and stop bubbling (watch them through the oven window, if you have one). Let cookies cool on the cookie sheet for a couple of minutes before carefully sliding them onto a rack to cool completely.

If you want (and why wouldn't you?), drizzle the cooled cookies with melted semisweet chocolate. Or just leave them plain. Either way they're delicious.

Makes about 5 dozen indescribably delicious cookies that will disappear instantly.

Gluten-Free Friendly
Substitute gluten-free all-purpose flour for the regular all-purpose flour in this recipe. Results may differ slightly from the original version.

Plain and Simple Sugar Cookies

Cut out great big circles of dough using an empty coffee can and sprinkle with sugar before baking, for the ultimate in simple cookiness. Or cut into festive shapes (don't forget a hanging hole) to bake, decorate and hang on your Christmas tree. Suit yourself. They're your cookies now.

1 cup	(250 ml)	butter, softened
1½ cups	(375 ml)	granulated sugar
2		eggs
1 tsp.	(5 ml)	vanilla extract
4 cups	(1 liter)	all-purpose flour
1 tbsp.	(15 ml)	baking powder
¼ cup	(60 ml)	cream or evaporated milk

In a large bowl, beat together the butter and the sugar with an electric mixer until smooth. Add the eggs and vanilla, and continue beating until creamy. Stir in the flour and baking powder alternately with the evaporated milk to make a fairly stiff dough. Turn the dough out onto a lightly floured surface and knead a few times by hand to make it smooth and workable. Refrigerate for at least 10 minutes before using.

Preheat the oven to 350°F (180°C). Line one or two cookie sheets with parchment paper.

Cut the dough into 4 pieces. Working with 1 piece of dough at a time, roll it out on a lightly floured surface to an even thickness of ¼ inch (6 mm), dusting lightly with flour to keep the dough from sticking to the rolling pin. Cut out shapes with cookie cutters and place the shapes on the prepared baking sheet, at least 1 inch (2.5 cm) apart to allow for spreading. Bake for 13 to 15 minutes, until the cookies are very slightly browned on the bottom, but still light colored on top.

Makes 3 to 4 dozen cookies, depending on what sizes you make.

But they're too plain!

✓ Brush unbaked cookies lightly with beaten egg white, milk or cream and sprinkle with plain or colored decorating sugar before baking.

✓ Decorate baked cookies elaborately with white or colored Royal Decorator Icing (see page 172).

✓ Glaze the tops of baked and cooled cookies with Shiny Sugar Glaze (see page 173) or Chocolate Ganache Glaze (see page 171). Add sprinkles (if you must) while the glaze is still wet.

✓ Or glaze half of each cookie with Shiny Sugar Glaze and Chocolate Ganache Glaze for a classic New York black-and-white cookie.

✓ Mix a few drops of liquid or paste food coloring into a beaten egg yolk and paint lovely designs on plain sugar cookies before baking.

Almost Authentic Scottish Shortbread

You don't have to go all the way to Loch Ness for delicious Scottish shortbread cookies. Unless, of course, you want to.

1 cup	(250 ml)	unsalted butter (please don't use margarine for this unless you have a very good reason)
½ cup	(125 ml)	icing sugar
2 cups	(500 ml)	flour
½ tsp.	(2 ml)	vanilla extract
¼ tsp.	(1 ml)	salt

In a large bowl, with an electric mixer, beat together the butter and the icing sugar until well blended. Add the flour, vanilla and salt, and blend into a smooth dough. Wrap dough in plastic wrap and refrigerate for 30 minutes to 1 hour. If you chill the dough any longer, it will harden and be difficult to shape. (But even if it does harden, just leave it out at room temperature until it softens up a bit.)

Preheat the oven to 350°F (180°C). Line one or two cookie sheets with parchment paper.

By hand, roll the dough into 1-inch (2 cm) balls and arrange them on the prepared cookie sheet. Flatten slightly to a thickness of about ½ inch (1 cm) using the bottom of a glass (that has been dipped in flour to prevent sticking). Prick a few fork holes in each cookie before baking, for an authentic shortbread effect. Bake for 12 to 14 minutes, until the bottoms of the cookies are lightly browned.

Makes about 3 dozen almost authentic shortbread cookies.

Four Inauthentic (but Genuinely Delicious) Shortbread Variations

There are those who might object to taking liberties with something as sacred as Scottish shortbread. Then again, there are those who wouldn't object at all.

Chocolate Chunk Shortbread

Add 1 cup (250 ml) coarsely chopped semisweet or bittersweet chocolate to the dough before chilling. Or use chocolate chips (if you must). Shape into balls, flatten slightly (as usual) and bake as if normal shortbread. Deadly.

Lemon or Orange Shortbread

Add 1 tbsp. (15 ml) finely grated lemon or orange peel to the dough before chilling. Shape and bake as usual.

Butter Pecan Shortbread

Omit icing sugar from the basic recipe, and use brown sugar instead. Add 1 cup (250 ml) ground pecans and 2 tsp. (10 ml) vanilla extract along with the flour. Shape and bake as usual.

Double Ginger Shortbread

Add 1 tsp. (5 ml) ground ginger and ¼ cup (60 ml) chopped crystallized ginger to the basic shortbread recipe. Shape and bake as usual.

Savory Rosemary and Parmesan Shortbread

These are the perfect little thing to serve with a wedge of cheese, a bowl of olives and a glass of wine. Be careful — they're habit-forming.

¾ cup	(175 ml)	butter, softened
2 tsp.	(10 ml)	sugar
2 cups	(500 ml)	all-purpose flour
¾ cup	(175 ml)	grated Parmesan cheese
2 tbsp.	(30 ml)	chopped fresh rosemary (or 2 tsp./10 ml crumbled dried)
½ tsp.	(2 ml)	paprika
¼ tsp.	(1 ml)	salt

In a medium-size bowl, beat together the butter and the sugar with an electric mixer until creamy. Stir in the flour, Parmesan, rosemary, paprika and salt, and mix until a stiff dough forms. The dough may be crumbly — that's okay; just smush it as much as possible until it sticks together. Divide the dough in 2 pieces. Roll each piece into a 12-inch (30 cm) long rope, about 1 inch (2 cm) thick. Wrap in plastic wrap or waxed paper and refrigerate for about 1 hour, until firm.

Preheat the oven to 350°F (180°C). Line one or two cookie sheets with parchment paper.

With a very sharp knife, cut the dough into ¼-inch (0.5 cm) slices and arrange on the cookie sheets. Bake for 13 to 15 minutes, or until very lightly browned on the bottom. Remove to a rack and let cool completely before serving.

Makes about 5 dozen tasty little thingamawhats.

Gingerbread People

Is there a better way to spend a cold winter afternoon than making a colony of gingerbread people? And it doesn't have to be just people. After all, dump trucks can be festive too.

1 cup	(250 ml)	granulated sugar
½ cup	(125 ml)	molasses
½ cup	(125 ml)	solid vegetable shortening, melted (not butter or margarine)
1		egg
1½ tsp.	(7 ml)	baking soda
2½ cups	(625 ml)	all-purpose flour
¼ tsp.	(1 ml)	ground ginger
1 tsp.	(5 ml)	cinnamon

In a large bowl, mix the sugar, molasses, melted shortening, egg and baking soda. Beat well with an electric mixer.

In another bowl, stir together the flour, ginger and cinnamon. Add the flour mixture gradually to the egg mixture, blending well. Cover the bowl with plastic wrap and chill the dough for several hours or overnight.

When you're ready to bake, preheat the oven to 350°F (180°C). Line one or two cookie sheets with parchment paper.

Cut the dough into about 4 pieces and roll each piece into a nice compact ball, flouring it well. Working with 1 ball of dough at a time, roll it out on a well-floured surface to a thickness of about ⅛ inch (3 mm). Using cookie cutters or your own original cardboard patterns, cut out gingerbread people (or animals, or dump trucks, or whatchamacallits). Carefully transfer the shapes to the prepared cookie sheets, leaving about 1 inch (2 cm) between them. Bake for 5 to 7 minutes, until very lightly browned around the edges. Watch closely — small shapes will bake more quickly than large ones will.

Let cookies cool for a minute or two before removing them to a rack to cool completely. Decorate with Royal Decorator Icing (see page 172).

Makes a lot of people (or animals, aliens, dump trucks and so on) or one phenomenal gingerbread house (see page 102).

Whole Wheat Positive
You can substitute whole wheat flour for all or part of the all-purpose flour in this recipe. Start with a small proportion, and if you like the result, you can use more whole wheat flour next time.

Gingerbread House

Melted Sugar Glue

Measure about 1 cup (250 ml) of sugar into a heavy skillet. Place over medium heat and cook, stirring occasionally, until the sugar melts and liquefies — this will take about 5 to 10 minutes. Don't try to hurry the process — sugar burns very easily. Reduce the heat to ultra-low to keep the sugar glue liquefied throughout the construction process. Be careful handling it because melted sugar is screamingly hot.

Start with a batch of the same dough that you used for Gingerbread People, but this time you're making building materials. No, really — it'll be fun.

You'll need:
  1 recipe Gingerbread People dough (see page 101)
  1 recipe Royal Decorator Icing (see page 172)
  a 12-inch (30 cm) square slab of rigid Styrofoam, ½ inch (1 cm) thick
  melted sugar glue (see sidebar)
  cardboard pattern (see page 101)
  toothpicks (for temporary support)
  decorating stuff galore: candies, pretzels, cereal, licorice, gumdrops, and so on, and so on, and so on

Phase one: bake the pieces

Follow all the directions for making Gingerbread People, but instead of cutting the rolled dough out into, well, people shapes, cut around the cardboard pattern pieces to make house sections (see page 104). This recipe makes enough for all the house pieces, plus one extra roof piece, front piece and sidepiece. Because, well, accidents happen. Transfer pieces to the prepared cookie sheet very carefully so as not to warp them (use a wide spatula or cardboard pattern to help lift the unbaked cutouts).

Bake pieces as for Gingerbread People, then let cool completely.

Phase two: construction

Have ready a few toothpicks (these can be used for temporary support, if needed), the Styrofoam base and a batch of melted sugar glue (see sidebar). Okay, let's begin.

Working as quickly as possible, dip the bottom and side edges of one wall piece into the melted sugar and stand it upright in position on the Styrofoam base. Do the same with the adjoining piece, making sure the pieces stick together at the corners. Repeat until you have the four walls standing upright. Now the roof: use a knife to spread melted sugar glue along the top edges of the house walls. Place a roof piece in position, then press it down gently so that it sticks. Repeat with the other roof section, sticking both roof sections together with dabs of melted sugar along the top. (Don't worry about drips. They're edible. Besides, you can hide them with icing later.) Assemble the chimney, hang the door and shutters, pour yourself a cup of coffee (or whatever) and take a breather. The worst is over.

Phase three: decoration

Now, far be it from me to tell you how to decorate this fabulous creation, but perhaps I can offer some suggestions.

- ✓ Use Royal Decorator Icing to detail the house and to stick on candies, or whatever else you're using.
- ✓ Drip Royal Decorator Icing from the edge of the roof to make realistic icicles.
- ✓ Use pretzel sticks to make good fences.
- ✓ Add marshmallows for very convincing snowmen.
- ✓ Use shredded wheat cereal and create a charming thatched roof.
- ✓ Donate your chewy, green spearmint leaf-shaped candies to use for some handy landscaping.
- ✓ Make cotton smoke curls for the chimney, of course.

Advanced Gingerbread Building Techniques

Those suggestions are too conventional, you say? Not creative enough for you? Too — ack! — suburban?

Well, smarty-pants, here's a challenge for you. Instead of cutting out traditional house pieces (as in the diagram), try baking an assortment of "lumber." You know — two-by-fours, planks, small sections of "drywall," doors — the kind of thing you'd get at Home Depot. Only, edible. Then, with a rough plan in mind, use the pieces to build your gingerbread creation. (Sort of like the way your crazy Uncle Louie built his garage a few years ago.)

Try building a treehouse using a real branch mounted on a wooden base for a "tree," with a rope ladder (string and pretzels) leading to the ground. Or make a rustic cabin, complete with front porch and outhouse. Whatever.

Have fun building — but don't forget to eat the house. Because next year, you'll make an even better one.

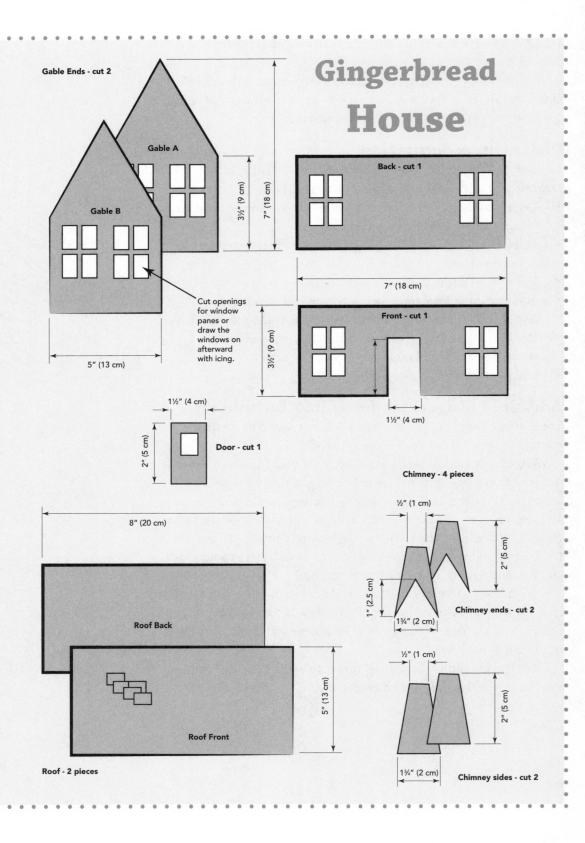

Gable Ends - cut 2

Gable A

Gable B

7" (18 cm)

3½" (9 cm)

5" (13 cm)

Cut openings for window panes or draw the windows on afterward with icing.

Gingerbread House

Back - cut 1

7" (18 cm)

Front - cut 1

3½" (9 cm)

1½" (4 cm)

1½" (4 cm)

2" (5 cm)

Door - cut 1

Chimney - 4 pieces

½" (1 cm)

2" (5 cm)

1" (2.5 cm)

1¾" (2 cm)

Chimney ends - cut 2

8" (20 cm)

Roof Back

5" (13 cm)

Roof Front

Roof - 2 pieces

½" (1 cm)

2" (5 cm)

1¾" (2 cm)

Chimney sides - cut 2

Giant Cookie Pizza

Here's a great thing to make with a bunch of kids (or, ahem, adults) on a rainy afternoon. Hold the pepperoni. Hold the anchovies. But definitely don't hold the chocolate chips.

1 cup	(250 ml)	butter
½ cup	(125 ml)	granulated sugar
½ cup	(125 ml)	brown sugar
1		egg
1 tsp.	(5 ml)	vanilla extract
1¾ cups	(425 ml)	all-purpose flour
1 cup	(250 ml)	semisweet chocolate chips
1 cup	(250 ml)	miniature marshmallows
1 cup	(250 ml)	peanuts or coarsely chopped walnuts

Preheat the oven to 375°F (190°C). Line a 14-inch (35 cm) pizza pan with parchment paper.

In a large bowl, beat together the butter, granulated sugar, brown sugar, egg and vanilla with an electric mixer until creamy. Measure in the flour, and beat until dough is smooth.

Dump the dough onto the prepared pizza pan and spread it out with a spatula, smoothing the dough right to the edges of the pan. Bake for 12 minutes.

Remove the partially baked crust from the oven, and sprinkle evenly with chocolate chips, marshmallows and nuts, leaving a naked border around the edge — for a realistic pizza crust effect. You might want to try other toppings too — gumdrops, shredded coconut, whatever — but keep the toppings to no more than 3 cups (750 ml) in total.

Return the pizza to the oven and bake for another 6 to 8 minutes, until the marshmallows are puffed and lightly browned. Let cool (at least partly, anyway), then cut into wedges and serve.

Makes one 14-inch (35 cm) pizza.

Whole Wheat Positive
You can substitute whole wheat flour for all or part of the all-purpose flour in this recipe. Start with a small proportion, and if you like the result, you can use more whole wheat flour next time.

Gluten-Free Friendly
Substitute gluten-free all-purpose flour for the regular all-purpose flour in this recipe. Results may differ slightly from the original version.

Four-Way Slice and Bake Cookies

This cookie is perfect for the indecisive person with sudden midnight cookie cravings. Keep a log or two in the freezer at all times so that it's available whenever the cookie urge hits.

Basic dough

1 cup	(250 ml)	butter
½ cup	(125 ml)	granulated sugar
½ cup	(125 ml)	brown sugar
1		egg
1 tsp.	(5 ml)	vanilla extract
2 cups	(500 ml)	all-purpose flour
½ tsp.	(2 ml)	baking soda

Add-in options (1 choice per ¼ recipe)

¼ cup	(60 ml)	chopped raisins
¼ cup	(60 ml)	chopped dried cranberries
¼ cup	(60 ml)	chopped pecans or walnuts
¼ cup	(60 ml)	chocolate sprinkles
¼ cup	(60 ml)	colored sprinkles
¼ cup	(60 ml)	shredded coconut
1 square		(1 oz./28 g) semisweet chocolate, melted

In a large bowl, beat together the butter, granulated sugar and brown sugar with an electric mixer until creamy. Beat in the egg and the vanilla. Add the flour and the baking soda, and mix thoroughly to form a soft dough.

Divide the dough into 4 equal portions and place in 4 separate bowls. Into each portion, add 1 of the above options — you can choose a different ingredient for each portion, if you like. Mix the addition into the dough until it is evenly blended. (Of course you can simply add 1 flavoring ingredient to the entire batch of dough — just increase the amount you're adding accordingly.) And you can always just leave the dough plain, if you're that type of person.

Gently roll each portion of dough into a log approximately 1¼ inches (4 cm) thick, then wrap it in waxed paper and refrigerate or freeze for at least several hours or overnight.

When you're ready to bake the cookies, preheat the oven to 375°F (190°C). Line one or two cookie sheets with parchment paper.

Unwrap each log and, with a very sharp knife, slice it into rounds ¼ inch (6 mm) thick. Place slices on the prepared cookie sheet and bake for 8 to 10 minutes, until lightly browned around the edges. Remove to a rack to cool.

Makes 5½ to 6 dozen cookies.

Hamantaschen

A traditional cookie for the Jewish holiday of Purim, these are incredibly easy and fun to make. Fill them with any kind of jam or canned pie filling, or stuff them with chocolate chips. Better yet, make some of everything. This recipe requires the use of a food processor.

1		medium seedless orange
2		eggs
¾ cup	(175 ml)	granulated sugar
½ cup	(125 ml)	vegetable oil
2¾ cups	(650 ml)	all-purpose flour
2 tsp.	(10 ml)	baking powder
		jam, prepared pie filling or chocolate chips

Preheat the oven to 350°F (180°C). Line one or two cookie sheets with parchment paper and grease the paper.

Cut the orange into quarters and place in the bowl of a food processor. Process, using quick on-off pulses, until the orange is finely chopped. Add the eggs, sugar and oil, and process for about 10 seconds. Scrape down the sides of the container, add the flour and baking powder, and process just until the flour is blended into dough. It will be soft and sticky, but that's okay.

Divide the dough into 2 or 3 portions and dust each one with flour. Roll each portion out on a well-floured surface to a thickness of about ⅛ inch (30 mm). Using a 3-inch (7 cm) round cookie cutter (or a drinking glass or whatever you have handy), cut the dough into circles. (You can gather up the scraps and reroll them, until you've used up all the dough.)

In the middle of each circle, put about ½ tsp. (2 ml) of jam or other filling. Pinch up the edge of each circle firmly in 3 places, making a triangular enclosure and leaving the top slightly open so that you can see the filling inside. Be sure the corners are tightly pinched to avoid unsightly leakage.

Place hamantaschen on the prepared cookie sheet and bake for 20 to 25 minutes, or until lightly browned.

Makes about 4 dozen.

Raspberry and Hazelnut Thumbprint Cookies

These are fun to make and pretty darn adorable. If you don't have hazelnuts, you can use almonds instead. And if you don't have raspberry jam, fill the cookies with whatever jam you do happen to have in the house. You'll need a food processor to make these.

1½ cups	(375 ml)	whole hazelnuts, divided
⅓ cup	(75 ml)	granulated sugar
¾ cup	(175 ml)	butter
1 tsp.	(5 ml)	vanilla extract
1¾ cups	(400 ml)	all-purpose flour
¼ cup	(60 ml)	raspberry (or other) jam

Preheat the oven to 350°F (180°C). Line a cookie sheet with parchment paper.

Measure 1 cup (250 ml) of the hazelnuts into a pie pan or other shallow baking pan. Place in the oven and bake for 15 minutes, or until the nuts are lightly toasted. Wrap the hot nuts in a clean dish towel, and roll them back and forth in your hands to rub the skins off. Remove the nuts from the towel — they should be mostly de-skinned (don't worry about the few stubborn skins that remain stuck). Set the nuts aside to cool.

While the toasted nuts are cooling, finely chop the remaining untoasted nuts in a food processor. Remove to a plate and set aside.

When the nuts are cool, place them in the container of the food processor and add the sugar. Process until the nuts and sugar are finely ground together. Add the butter and vanilla, and process until creamy. Add the flour and process the mixture until it forms a dough that can be easily handled.

By hand, form the dough into 1-inch (2 cm) balls. One at a time, roll each ball in the plate of chopped nuts until more or less coated, and place on the prepared cookie sheet. With a finger, thumb or the end of a wooden spoon, make an indentation in each cookie and fill it with a small dab of jam. Bake for 18 to 20 minutes, or until cookies are very lightly browned on the bottom. Transfer to a rack to cool.

Makes 3 dozen cookies.

Chocolate Walnut Rugelach

These are halfway between a cookie and a pastry. They look like a lot more work than they actually are. Very impressive.

1 recipe		**Rich Cream Cheese Pastry (page 180)**
⅓ cup	**(75 ml)**	**chocolate chips**
⅓ cup	**(75 ml)**	**chopped walnuts**
¼ cup	**(60 ml)**	**granulated sugar**
½ tsp.	**(2 ml)**	**cinnamon**
		icing sugar for dusting

Preheat the oven to 350°F (180°C). Line one or two cookie sheets with parchment paper.

Prepare the Rich Cream Cheese Pastry dough and refrigerate for about 1 hour.

In the container of a food processor, combine the chocolate chips, walnuts, sugar and cinnamon, and process, using quick on-off pulses, until finely chopped.

Cut the ball of pastry dough into 4 pieces, and dust each one lightly with flour. On a lightly floured surface, roll out 1 ball of dough into a circle, approximately 10 inches (25 cm) in diameter. Handle the dough gently, and don't be afraid to sprinkle it with more flour to prevent the dough from sticking to the counter or the rolling pin. Sprinkle the entire surface of this circle evenly with ¼ of the filling. Using a pizza cutter (or a sharp knife), cut the circle into 8 wedges — pizza style. Roll up each wedge — starting at the wide, outside edge — rolling firmly toward the point. Place on an ungreased cookie sheet and bend each one slightly to form a crescent. There — aren't they cute? Repeat with the rest of the dough and the remaining filling.

Bake for 15 to 20 minutes, until very lightly browned on top and lightly browned on the bottom. Watch carefully because they can burn quickly. Remove to a rack to cool, then dust with icing sugar before serving.

Makes exactly 32 rugelach.

Dog Biscuits

Thoroughly dog tested and deemed woofworthy by our panel of canine experts. These biscuits taste almost as good as week-old dead groundhog. Or so I've been told.

3 cups	(750 ml)	whole wheat flour
2 cups	(500 ml)	quick-cooking rolled oats (not instant)
¼ cup	(60 ml)	wheat germ
¼ cup	(60 ml)	skim milk powder
½ tsp.	(2 ml)	garlic powder
1¼ cups	(300 ml)	water
⅓ cup	(75 ml)	peanut butter
1		egg

Preheat the oven to 300°F (150°C). Line a cookie sheet or two with parchment paper.

In a large bowl, mix the flour, oats, wheat germ, milk powder and garlic powder. In the container of a blender or food processor, blend the water, peanut butter and egg until smooth. Add the egg mixture to the flour mixture and stir to make a stiff dough.

Working with half of the dough at a time, roll the dough out on a lightly floured surface to thickness of about ½ inch (1 cm). (The biscuits are supposed to be chunky.) Cut into shapes with cookie cutters. Dog-bone shapes are a logical choice, but your dog may prefer letter carriers, squirrels or, uh, cats. Place on the prepared cookie sheet and bake for 1 to 1½ hours, until hard and crunchy. (Use the shorter baking time if you want a slightly softer biscuit.)

Makes about 3 or 4 dozen, depending on the size.

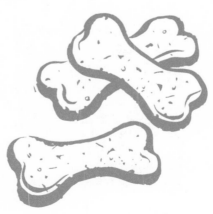

Nonedible Cookies

Interesting Effect

Work some paste food coloring (not liquid) into the dough before rolling it out. If you mush it in with your hands, you can get a very neat marbelized effect. You can find paste food coloring in any store that sells serious cake-decorating supplies. It's superconcentrated and produces vibrant colors. (Great for tinting frosting too.)

So, you might wonder, what's the point? Well, for one thing, these make very cool Christmas tree decorations. Spray-paint them silver or gold; decorate them with water-based paint and coat them with urethane; or just go crazy with glitter and glue and whatever you can find. This is art — you don't need a point.

2 cups	**(500 ml)**	**all-purpose flour**
1 cup	**(250 ml)**	**salt**
1 cup	**(250 ml)**	**water**

Preheat the oven to 250°F (120°C). Line a cookie sheet or two with parchment paper and grease the paper lightly.

Combine flour and salt in a bowl, and mix well. Add the water, a bit at a time, and mix well, until the dough forms a ball and is easy to handle. You may not need to add all the water if the dough seems soft enough, so don't dump all the water in at once. Knead the dough on a lightly floured surface until smooth — about 5 minutes or so.

Roll the dough out about ¼ inch (0.5 cm) thick on a lightly floured surface. Cut into shapes with cookie cutters (or whatever you want) and place on the prepared cookie sheet(s). Bake for 35 to 40 minutes, until the, um, whatchamacallits are firm and dry. Let cool, then decorate them in whatever wild and wonderful way you like.

Makes about 25 medium shapes, and they last practically forever. Which is a good thing because this is, after all, art.

Squares and Bars

Easy Saucepan Brownies

Here's a good basic brownie that's delicious and ridiculously easy to make. Sprinkle with icing sugar for a simple finishing touch, or spread with frosting for a more serious chocolate impact.

⅓ cup	(75 ml)	butter
⅔ cup	(150 ml)	granulated sugar
1 cup	(250 ml)	chocolate chips
2 tbsp.	(30 ml)	water
2		eggs
¾ cup	(175 ml)	all-purpose flour
½ tsp.	(2 ml)	baking powder
1 tsp.	(5 ml)	vanilla extract
½ cup	(125 ml)	coarsely chopped walnuts (optional)

Preheat the oven to 350°F (180°C). Grease an 8 or 9-inch (20 or 23 cm) square baking pan.

In a medium saucepan, combine the butter, sugar, chocolate chips and water. Place over low heat and cook, stirring constantly, just until the chocolate is melted and the mixture is smooth. Remove from heat and let cool for a couple of minutes.

Add the eggs to the chocolate mixture and whisk until smooth. Dump in the flour, baking powder and vanilla, and stir just until the dry ingredients have been incorporated, then add the chopped walnuts and stir to mix. Pour into the prepared baking pan and bake for 25 to 30 minutes — until a toothpick poked into the middle comes out nearly clean. If you're not quite sure, then they're done.

Makes 16 to 25 brownies.

Two-Bite Brownies

Use this recipe to make a batch of little weensy individual brownies just like the ones they sell at the store. Better, actually. Warning: they're seriously addictive.

Prepare batter using the recipe here, but omit the nuts. Spoon the batter into a well-greased miniature muffin pan (1 heaping teaspoonful of batter in each cup). Bake at 350°F (180°C) for 10 to 12 minutes.

Makes about 48 individual brownies.

Gluten-Free Friendly
Substitute gluten-free all-purpose flour for the regular all-purpose flour in this recipe. Results may differ slightly from the original version.

Dastardly Double Fudge Brownies

Ack! I wrecked my chocolate!

Did you splash water into the chocolate you were melting? And now you're sorry — it's all seized up into icky, clumpy bits that will not go away. Disaster? Well, maybe or maybe not. Here's how you may still be able to rescue your ruined chocolate:

For each 1 oz. (28 g) square of chocolate (or equivalent amount of chocolate chips) that has been tragically wrecked, add 1 tsp. (5 ml) vegetable oil or solid vegetable shortening. Place over very low heat and stir until it smooths out. You hope. (Don't use butter or margarine to do this because both contain water and will only make matters worse.) If it doesn't work, you probably have to toss the chocolate and try again.

Just be more careful next time — will you, please?

These brownies are thick, fudgy and positively dastardly. They really need no frosting, but if you insist, you can slather them with Chocolate Ganache Glaze (page 171) or Chocolate Buttercream Frosting (page 166) when they're completely cool. Like they'll last that long.

4 squares		(1 oz./28 g each) unsweetened chocolate
¾ cup	(175 ml)	butter
1½ cups	(375 ml)	granulated sugar
3		eggs
2 tsp.	(10 ml)	vanilla extract
¾ cup	(175 ml)	all-purpose flour
½ cup	(125 ml)	semisweet chocolate chips
½ cup	(125 ml)	chopped walnuts (optional)

Preheat the oven to 350°F (180°C). Grease an 8 or 9-inch (20 or 23 cm) square baking pan.

In a medium-size saucepan, melt together the chocolate and the butter over low heat, stirring occasionally until the mixture is smooth. Remove from heat and let cool slightly.

With a whisk (or with an electric mixer), beat in the sugar, then add the eggs and vanilla, and continue beating until smooth. Stir in the flour and mix just until it disappears into the batter. Add the chocolate chips and walnuts (if you're using them), mix well and transfer to the prepared baking pan. Bake for 35 to 40 minutes, until set but not dry (a toothpick poked into the middle of the pan should come out with a little bit of chocolaty stuff clinging to it). Don't overbake — it will ruin the fudgy effect.

Makes one 8 or 9-inch (20 or 23 cm) pan of perfectly dastardly brownies, 16 to 25 brownies.

Gluten-Free Friendly
Substitute gluten-free all-purpose flour for the regular all-purpose flour in this recipe. Results may differ slightly from the original version.

Marbled Peanut Butter Brownies

Chocolate and peanut butter. Together at last. In one brownie. A match made in heaven.

½ cup	(125 ml)	butter
¼ cup	(60 ml)	smooth peanut butter
1 tsp.	(5 ml)	vanilla extract
1 cup	(250 ml)	granulated sugar
1 cup	(250 ml)	brown sugar
3		eggs
2 cups	(500 ml)	all-purpose flour
2 tsp.	(10 ml)	baking powder
½ cup	(125 ml)	chocolate syrup (the regular chocolate milk kind)

Preheat the oven to 350°F (180°C). Grease a 9 x 13-inch (23 x 33 cm) baking pan.

In a large bowl, beat together the butter, peanut butter and vanilla with an electric mixer until creamy. Add the granulated sugar and the brown sugar, and beat well. Now add the eggs, 1 at a time, continuing to beat the mixture until fluffy.

In another bowl, stir together the flour and the baking powder. Add this to the peanut butter mixture and mix well.

Spread half of the batter in the prepared baking dish. Drizzle the chocolate syrup over the batter, then top with the remaining batter. (The top layer of batter may not spread easily over the chocolate syrup. Just glop it on as well as you can — it'll be fine; you'll see.) Swirl the mixture by running a knife through the batter several times to create a marbled effect. Don't overswirl — you wouldn't want to ruin the marbled effect. Bake for 35 to 40 minutes, until lightly browned. Let cool before cutting into squares.

Makes about 24 to 25 swirly brownies.

Nanaimo Bars

Okay, so they're not actually baked. But let's just ignore that technicality — these wicked little treats definitely belong in this book. They're easy to make, completely irresistible and can hold their own on any cookie plate.

Bottom layer

½ cup	(125 ml)	butter
⅓ cup	(75 ml)	unsweetened cocoa powder
¼ cup	(60 ml)	granulated sugar
1		egg, lightly beaten
2 cups	(500 ml)	graham cracker crumbs
1 cup	(250 ml)	unsweetened shredded coconut
½ cup	(125 ml)	chopped walnuts
1 tsp.	(5 ml)	vanilla extract

Middle layer

¼ cup	(60 ml)	butter, softened
2 cups	(500 ml)	icing sugar
3 tbsp.	(45 ml)	milk or cream
2 tbsp.	(30 ml)	instant vanilla pudding powder
½ tsp.	(2 ml)	vanilla extract

Topping

4 squares		(1 oz./28 g each) semisweet chocolate
1 tbsp.	(15 ml)	butter

Lightly grease an 8 or 9-inch (20 or 23 cm) square baking pan.

First, make the bottom layer. Melt the butter in a saucepan over low heat. Remove the pan from heat and stir in the cocoa powder and sugar, mixing until smooth. Return the pan to heat and add the egg, whisking until the mixture thickens slightly. Remove from heat and stir in the graham cracker crumbs, coconut, walnuts and vanilla. Mix well. Dump this mixture into the prepared pan and press it evenly in a layer on the bottom of the pan. Refrigerate until firm — about 1 hour.

Now make the middle layer. In a large bowl, beat the butter with an electric mixer until creamy. Add the icing sugar, milk or cream, pudding powder and vanilla, and beat until the mixture is very smooth and creamy. Spread this over the chilled bottom layer, smoothing the top as much as possible. Return to the refrigerator until firm — 30 minutes to 1 hour.

Finally, the topping. Chop the chocolate into pieces and place in a small saucepan with the butter. Place over low heat, stirring just until smooth and melted. Working very quickly, pour the melted chocolate over the creamy layer and spread it out as evenly and smoothly as possible. You don't want the warm chocolate to melt the icing mixture, so you'll have to be a little careful here. Cover with plastic wrap and refrigerate just until the chocolate is set.

To serve, cut into small squares with a very sharp knife. (It's easiest to do this before the chocolate has fully hardened.) Once cut, Nanaimo Bars should be allowed to chill in the pan until completely firm before removing them to a plate.

Makes 25 to 36 squares.

Butterscotch Granola Blondies

Load 'em up!

Go ahead — add some extra, um, nutritional kick to these blondies, if you want. Stir in ½ cup (125 ml) each dried cranberries and semisweet chocolate chips along with the granola.

Use any old kind of granola you happen to have in the house to make these chewy, delicious bars. They're even good with that stale, leftover stuff from the bottom of the box.

1 cup	**(250 ml)**	**brown sugar, packed**
¼ cup	**(60 ml)**	**vegetable oil**
1		**egg**
2 tsp.	**(10 ml)**	**vanilla extract**
¾ cup	**(175 ml)**	**all-purpose flour**
1 tsp.	**(5 ml)**	**baking powder**
1 cup	**(250 ml)**	**granola cereal (any kind)**

Preheat the oven to 350°F (180°C). Grease an 8 or 9-inch (20 or 23 cm) square baking pan.

In a medium bowl, combine the brown sugar, oil, egg and vanilla. Beat or whisk together until well mixed. Add the flour, baking powder and granola, and stir just until the dry ingredients have been incorporated into the batter. It will be thick.

Spread batter in the prepared baking pan and bake for 25 to 30 minutes. Cut into squares while still warm.

Makes 16 to 25 blondies.

Whole Wheat Positive
You can substitute whole wheat flour for all or part of the all-purpose flour in this recipe. Start with a small proportion, and if you like the result, you can use more whole wheat flour next time.

Gluten-Free Friendly
Substitute gluten-free all-purpose flour for the regular all-purpose flour in this recipe. Results may differ slightly from the original version.

Chocolate Hazelnut Truffle Squares

These squares are brownies with delusions of grandeur. Dense and chocolaty, they should be cut into teensy squares for serving. As a bonus, they're gluten-free.

⅓ cup	(75 ml)	butter
2 squares		(1 oz./28 g each) unsweetened chocolate
1 cup	(250 ml)	granulated sugar
3		eggs
2 tsp.	(10 ml)	vanilla extract
1½ cups	(375 ml)	finely chopped hazelnuts

Preheat oven to 325°F (160°C). Grease an 8 or 9-inch (20 or 23 cm) square baking pan.

In a medium saucepan, melt together the butter and the chocolate over low heat, stirring until smooth. Remove from heat and stir in the sugar, eggs and vanilla. Beat with an electric mixer or whisk until blended, then stir in the hazelnuts. Mix thoroughly, then spread batter evenly into the prepared baking pan. Bake for 40 to 45 minutes, until set. (A toothpick poked into the middle of the dish should come out more or less clean.)

Let cool completely before cutting into tiny squares. Store truffle squares in a covered container in the refrigerator.

Makes about 36 outrageously rich little squares.

Let's have a toast!

Toasting nuts to use in a recipe makes them crunchier and gives them a deeper, richer nutty flavor. Hazelnuts, almonds and walnuts especially benefit from a bit of toasting. Here's how to do it.

Preheat the oven to 350°F (180°C). Spread the nuts on an ungreased baking pan and place in the oven for 10 to 15 minutes, stirring them every 5 minutes, until they're lightly browned and fragrant. Make sure you don't forget about them, because they can go from perfectly toasted to scorched in about two minutes. Let cool to room temperature before using. Always toast a few more nuts than your recipe calls for to make up for shrinkage and snack-age.

Survival Bars

Don't you just hate it when you get lost in the jungle? Well, at least you won't starve if you remember to pack a few of these in your knapsack. Also good for less dire (but equally stressful) situations — like school lunches.

3		eggs
¾ cup	(175 ml)	granulated sugar
¾ cup	(175 ml)	whole wheat flour
¼ cup	(60 ml)	wheat germ
1 cup	(250 ml)	chocolate chips
1 cup	(250 ml)	chopped walnuts
1 cup	(250 ml)	shredded unsweetened coconut
1 cup	(250 ml)	chopped dates or dried figs

Preheat the oven to 350°F (180°C). Grease an 8 or 9-inch (20 or 23 cm) square baking pan.

In a large bowl, with an electric mixer, beat the eggs with the sugar for 2 or 3 minutes, until light and creamy. Stir in the flour and the wheat germ, and mix well. Add the chocolate chips, walnuts, coconut and dates or figs. Mix well and pour into the prepared baking pan. Bake for 25 to 30 minutes, until lightly browned on the edges. Let cool completely before cutting into squares with a very sharp knife.

Makes about 16 to 25 survival bars — enough to keep you alive for a couple of days at least.

Gluten-Free Friendly
Substitute gluten-free all-purpose flour for the regular all-purpose flour in this recipe. Results may differ slightly from the original version.

Zingy Lemon Squares

What we have here is a serious lemon hit. Perfect (perfect!) with a cup of tea, these are elegant and irresistible.

Shortbread base

2 cups	(500 ml)	all-purpose flour
¾ cup	(175 ml)	butter
½ cup	(125 ml)	icing sugar

Lemon topping

4		eggs
1½ cups	(375 ml)	granulated sugar
½ cup	(125 ml)	lemon juice
¼ cup	(60 ml)	all-purpose flour
1 tsp.	(5 ml)	baking powder
2 tsp.	(10 ml)	grated lemon zest (about 2 lemons' worth)
		Additional icing sugar for sprinkling on top

Nuke that lemon

To get the most juice from your lemon, zap it in the microwave for 10 seconds on high power before squeezing. The lemon will be easier to squeeze, and you'll get more juice. Just another one of life's little mysteries.

Preheat the oven to 350°F (180°C). Line the bottom of a 9 x 13-inch (23 x 33 cm) rectangular baking pan with parchment paper.

In a medium bowl, with a pastry blender, combine the flour, butter and icing sugar, mixing them into a crumbly mixture (don't worry about getting it to stick together). Press this mixture firmly and evenly into the bottom of the prepared baking pan. Bake for 20 minutes — just until the crust begins to set. Let cool for about 10 minutes.

In a large bowl, beat together the eggs, granulated sugar and lemon juice. Add the flour, baking powder and lemon zest, and beat until smooth. Pour over the baked base and return the pan to the oven. Bake for 25 minutes, until the topping is set and just beginning to brown around the edges. Let cool completely, then sprinkle with icing sugar and cut into squares.

Makes 24 to 35 squares.

Variations on a Lemon Square

Start with the shortbread base from Zingy Lemon Squares and have your way with it. Here are two excellent possibilities.

Butter Tart Squares

2¼ cups	(530 ml)	brown sugar
⅓ cup	(75 ml)	butter, melted
3		eggs
2 tbsp.	(30 ml)	vinegar
2 tsp.	(10 ml)	vanilla extract
1 cup	(250 ml)	raisins or chopped walnuts

Preheat the oven to 350°F (180°C). Prepare and prebake the shortbread base as for Zingy Lemon Squares.

Beat together the brown sugar, melted butter, eggs, vinegar and vanilla until blended. Sprinkle the raisins (or nuts) evenly over the prebaked base, then pour the brown sugar mixture over top. Bake for 25 to 30 minutes, until set. Let cool completely before cutting into squares.

Makes 24 to 35 squares.

Coconut Squares

3		eggs
2 cups	(500 ml)	brown sugar
3 tbsp.	(45 ml)	flour
2 tsp.	(10 ml)	baking powder
1½ cups	(375 ml)	chopped walnuts
1½ cups	(375 ml)	shredded unsweetened coconut

Preheat the oven to 350°F (180°C). Prepare and prebake the shortbread base as for Zingy Lemon Squares.

In a large bowl, with an electric mixer, beat together the eggs and the brown sugar for about 5 minutes, until thickened. Stir in the flour and baking powder, and mix well. Add the walnuts and coconut, and stir to combine. Pour over partially baked base and bake for 30 to 35 minutes, or until set.

Cut into squares while still warm.

Crumbly Apple Squares

Crumbly is good. Make sure you have a napkin on your lap when you're eating these. Or use a plate.

1½ cups	(375 ml)	all-purpose flour
1½ cups	(375 ml)	quick-cooking rolled oats (not instant)
½ cup	(125 ml)	brown sugar
¾ cup	(175 ml)	butter
4		medium apples, peeled, cored and thinly sliced
2 tbsp.	(30 ml)	granulated sugar
1 tsp.	(5 ml)	lemon juice
½ tsp.	(2 ml)	cinnamon

Preheat the oven to 350°F (180°C). Grease an 8 or 9-inch (20 or 23 cm) square baking pan.

In a medium bowl, mix the flour, oats and brown sugar. Using a pastry blender or a fork, mix the butter into the flour mixture, mashing it up so it forms a crumbly mixture. You don't have to worry about being delicate here — just smush the butter into the dry ingredients until it disappears. Dump ⅔ of this mixture into the prepared baking pan. Press to form an even layer. Set aside the remaining crumble mixture.

In another bowl, toss together the sliced apples, granulated sugar, lemon juice and cinnamon. Spread over the flour mixture in the pan, patting the apples down into an even layer without any spaces. Sprinkle with the remaining crumble mixture, then press it firmly over the apples. Bake for 45 to 50 minutes, until the topping is lightly browned around the edges and the apples are tender when you (inconspicuously) poke into them with a knife. Let cool for at least 10 minutes before cutting into squares and serving with ice cream. They're also delicious without ice cream and at room temperature.

Makes 16 to 25 squares.

Whole Wheat Positive
You can substitute whole wheat flour for all or part of the all-purpose flour in this recipe. Start with a small proportion, and if you like the result, you can use more whole wheat flour next time.

Jam Squares

Instead of the apple filling, spread the prepared base with about 1½ cups (375 ml) of any type of jam (even a mixture of several different kinds). Proceed with the recipe as usual. Reduce the baking time to 30 to 35 minutes.

Cheesecake Squares

You want a little cheesecake. Just a bite. So here. Make these.

⅓ cup	(75 ml)	butter
⅓ cup	(75 ml)	brown sugar
1 cup	(250 ml)	all-purpose flour
½ cup	(125 ml)	chopped pecans
1 pkg.		(8 oz./250 g) cream cheese, softened
¼ cup	(60 ml)	granulated sugar
1		egg
1 tbsp.	(15 ml)	lemon juice
1 tsp.	(5 ml)	vanilla extract

Preheat the oven to 350°F (180°C). Have ready an 8 or 9-inch (20 or 23 cm) square baking pan, but don't grease it.

Beat together the butter and brown sugar in a medium bowl until creamy. Add the flour and pecans, and stir to make a crumbly mixture. Press half the flour mixture into the bottom of the prepared baking pan. (Set aside the remaining crumbs for later.) Bake the crust for 12 to 14 minutes, until just beginning to set at the edges. Remove from the oven and let cool for a few minutes while you prepare the filling.

In a large bowl, beat the cream cheese and sugar with an electric mixer until smooth. Add the egg, lemon juice and vanilla, and continue beating for another couple of minutes, until the mixture is creamy. Pour into the prebaked crust and sprinkle the top evenly with the reserved crumbs (remember them?). Bake for 25 to 30 minutes — until just set, but not yet browned. Let cool in pan before cutting into squares.

Makes about 16 to 25 squares. Just enough.

Gluten-Free Friendly
Substitute gluten-free all-purpose flour for the regular all-purpose flour in this recipe. Results may differ slightly from the original version.

Clueless Troubleshooting: Cookies and Squares

Did your good cookies turn out bad? It's a devastating experience. We know. We feel your pain. We want to help.

The cookies spread out too much on the baking sheet.

✓ There may have been too much butter or other shortening in the dough. Increase the flour next time or reduce the amount of shortening.

✓ The oven may not have been hot enough, causing the dough to splodge out before it set. Increase the temperature by 10 to 15 degrees and see what happens. (Check your oven temperature with a thermometer to see if it's accurate.)

✓ Was the cookie sheet warm from a previous batch? This can cause the dough to melt and spread before it actually begins baking. Cool the cookie sheet between batches or, better yet, use two sheets and alternate them.

The cookies were burned on the bottom.

✓ Is your oven temperature accurate? Check it with an oven thermometer.

✓ If the pan was on the bottom shelf in the oven, move it up to the middle or upper shelf. If you are baking two pans at once, switch them around halfway through the baking time so that they bake more evenly.

✓ Dark colored cookie sheets will brown the bottom of the cookies more quickly than shiny ones will. Use shiny baking sheets, if possible, or line your cookie sheets with foil.

Drat. The *$#@&#! Cookies stuck to the pan!

✓ Did you grease the cookie sheet or line it with parchment paper? See what happens?

✓ Next time, line your cookie sheets with parchment paper. You'll never have another stuck cookie — guaranteed. And you don't have to replace the paper for each batch of cookies. Just remove the baked cookies, wipe off any excess grease with a paper towel and keep right on baking.

The cookies were too hard when they cooled.
- ✓ They were overbaked. Cut down on the baking time by a couple of minutes next batch.
- ✓ Maybe there was too much flour in the dough. Reduce flour by a small amount and see if that helps.
- ✓ Put the cookies in a container with a tight-fitting lid and throw in a chunk of apple. Let them room together overnight and see what happens — it just might help.

The dough cracks when I try to roll it out.
- ✓ Too much flour. Reduce the amount of flour next time.
- ✓ Was the dough too cold? Let it warm up slightly (or knead it in your hands to soften it) before trying to roll it out.
- ✓ Add a teensy bit of liquid to the dough to make it pliable.

The cookie dough is too sticky.
- ✓ Add a bit more flour to make it workable and roll it out on a well-floured surface. Dust your rolling pin with flour too.
- ✓ Chill the dough for an hour or two before rolling. Then cut the dough into pieces and just roll a manageable portion of the dough at a time.

I wanted chewy brownies. These are crunchy.
- ✓ Always underbake brownies. When you think they might be done — they probably are. They'll continue to firm up as they cool, so if they're a little too soft when you take them out of the oven, they'll be just right.

Cakes and Frostings

It's your birthday? You need a cake. You passed your eye exam?
You need a cake. You got a new dog? It's cake time! A new friend?
A parking ticket? A promotion? Athlete's foot? An inheritance? If
you're happy, bake a cake to celebrate. If you're grumpy, a cake will
cheer you up. No matter how weird or wonderful the occasion, a cake
is just the thing you need. You don't have an occasion? Invent one.

Cakes

Perfectly Simple Chocolate Cake

Bigger takes longer

For complex scientific reasons, when you bake cake batter in one large pan — let's say 9 x 13 inches (23 x 33 cm) — the baking time will be slightly longer than for the same amount of batter in two smaller pans. The range of baking time indicated in the cake recipes cleverly takes this into account. Big pan, longer time. Small pan, shorter time. That's all there is to it.

Better than a cake from a mix and just as easy. Perfect.

2 cups	(500 ml)	all-purpose flour
2 cups	(500 ml)	granulated sugar
½ cup	(125 ml)	unsweetened cocoa powder
1 tsp.	(5 ml)	baking powder
1 tsp.	(5 ml)	baking soda
1½ cups	(375 ml)	milk
½ cup	(125 ml)	vegetable oil
1 tsp.	(5 ml)	vanilla extract
2		eggs

Preheat the oven to 350°F (180°C). Line two 8 or 9-inch (20 or 23 cm) round cake pans or one 9 x 13-inch (23 x 33 cm) rectangular cake pan with parchment paper. Grease the paper and the sides of the pan.

In a large mixing bowl, combine the flour, sugar, cocoa powder, baking powder and baking soda. Add the milk, vegetable oil and vanilla, and beat with an electric mixer for about 2 minutes, until smooth, scraping down the sides several times. Add the eggs and beat for another minute or two.

Pour batter evenly into the 2 round pans or into the single rectangular pan. Slam each pan against the counter once or twice to eliminate any large bubbles. Bake for 35 to 40 minutes, or until a toothpick poked into the middle of the cake comes out clean. Let cool in the pan for 5 minutes, then invert on a rack, peel off the paper and let cool completely before doing something delicious with it.

Makes two 8 or 9-inch (20 or 23 cm) round layers or one 9 x 13-inch (23 x 33 cm) rectangular cake.

Preparing a Cake Pan

This is, frankly, not all that much fun, but doing it right is definitely worthwhile. Do it first — before you begin mixing the batter or dough — so you won't be tempted to rush through this crucial task.

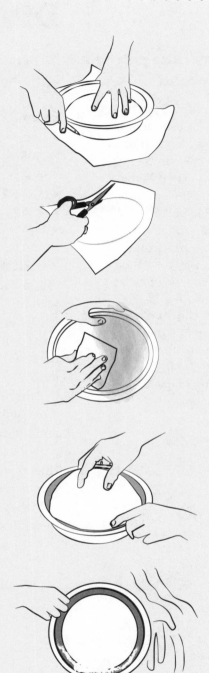

Cut a sheet of baker's parchment paper (see page 79) a little larger than your baking pan. Lay it on the counter, place the baking pan on top and, using a pencil, trace around the bottom of the pan. Cut along the lines and you now have a paper liner that will fit exactly into the bottom of your pan.

Next, using vegetable oil shortening or nonstick baking spray, lightly grease the bottom and sides of your baking pan. Place the paper liner in the bottom of the pan and smooth it out so that there are no wrinkles. Grease this paper liner and the sides of the pan again, and you are now ready to bake.

See? Aren't you happy that's over with?

Preparing a Cake Pan — an advanced technique

A recipe may tell you to "grease and flour" your pan. This is sometimes done with delicate cakes that are particularly prone to sticking. Here's what you do:

Prepare your cake pan as above (line the bottom with paper) and grease the bottom and sides really well. Now sprinkle in a small amount (1 tbsp./15 ml) of flour and tilt the pan around, tapping it so that the flour sticks evenly to all the inside surfaces of the pan. Dump out any excess flour, pour in the batter and bake as usual. If you're making a chocolate cake, you can use cocoa powder instead of flour so that it doesn't show.

Divine Yellow Cake

Any cake can be a cupcake

Any basic cake batter can be used to make cupcakes. Just spoon the cake batter into a paper-lined muffin pan, filling the cups about ½ full. Bake for half the time required to bake a full-size cake, then test with a toothpick to see if the cupcakes are done (see page 22). If not, continue baking for another 5 minutes or so, or until they're ready. Let cool completely before slathering with icing (of course).

Ridiculously easy, light and delicious — this cake can handle whatever you care to throw at it. Especially strawberries and whipped cream.

2 cups	**(500 ml)**	**granulated sugar**
4		**eggs**
¾ cup	**(175 ml)**	**vegetable oil**
1 cup	**(250 ml)**	**milk**
2½ cups	**(600 ml)**	**all-purpose flour**
2¼ tsp.	**(11 ml)**	**baking powder**
1 tsp.	**(5 ml)**	**vanilla extract**

Preheat the oven to 350°F (180°C). Line two 8 or 9-inch (20 or 23 cm) round cake pans or one 9 x 13-inch (23 x 33 cm) rectangular cake pan with parchment paper. Grease the paper and the sides of the pan.

In a large mixing bowl, beat the sugar and eggs with an electric mixer until slightly thickened — about 1 minute. Add the oil, milk, flour, baking powder and vanilla, and beat for another minute — just until the batter is smooth and creamy. Don't overbeat it.

Pour batter evenly into the two round pans or into the single rectangular pan. Bake for 30 to 35 minutes, until the tops are golden and a toothpick poked into the center of the layer comes out clean.

Run a knife around the sides of the cake to loosen it from the pan, then turn the cake out onto a rack, peel off the paper and let cool completely before having your way with it.

Makes two 8 or 9-inch (20 or 23 cm) round layers, or one 9 x 13-inch (23 x 33 cm) rectangular cake.

Classic Carrot Cake

Why would any sane person have put carrots in a cake? Was it an accident? A misprinted recipe? A joke? Never mind — the cake is a classic.

2 cups	(500 ml)	all-purpose flour
2 tsp.	(10 ml)	baking powder
1½ tsp.	(7 ml)	baking soda
1 tsp.	(5 ml)	cinnamon
2 cups	(500 ml)	granulated sugar
1 cup	(250 ml)	vegetable oil
4		eggs
2 cups	(500 ml)	grated carrots (about 3 medium carrots)
1 cup	(250 ml)	canned crushed pineapple, well drained
½ cup	(125 ml)	chopped walnuts or pecans

Preheat the oven to 350°F (180°C). Line two 8 or 9-inch (20 or 23 cm) round cake pans or one 9 x 13-inch (23 x 33 cm) rectangular cake pan with parchment paper. Grease the paper and the sides of the pan.

In a medium bowl, stir together the flour, baking powder, baking soda and cinnamon.

In a large bowl, beat the sugar, oil and eggs with an electric mixer until smooth. Add the flour mixture to the egg mixture and beat well. Stir in the carrots, pineapple and walnuts or pecans, mixing until blended. Pour batter into the prepared pans. Bake for 40 to 45 minutes, or until a toothpick poked into the middle of the cake comes out clean.

Run a knife around the sides of the cake to loosen it from the pan, then turn the layers out onto a rack. Peel off the paper and let cool completely before frosting with (what else?) Cream Cheese Frosting (see page 171).

Makes two 8 or 9 inch (20 or 23 cm) round layers or one 9 x 13-inch (23 x 33 cm) rectangular cake.

Red Velvet Cake

Redder velvet cake?

Like so many wonderful things, red velvet cake is capable of evoking some pretty intense controversy. Dark burgundy red? Bright cherry red? Something in between? This particular recipe produces a dark mahogany-red cake because of the relatively high proportion of cocoa in the batter. For a brighter, purer red color, reduce the amount of cocoa to ¼ cup (60 ml). Your cake will be less chocolaty, but still delicious. And very, very red.

It's not clear who came up with the goofy idea to dump a whole bottle of red food coloring into a basic cake batter, but it definitely makes for one outrageous cake! Add some Cream Cheese Frosting (page 171) and it's over the top. In the best possible way, of course.

1½ cups	(375 ml)	granulated sugar
½ cup	(125 ml)	vegetable oil
2		eggs
1 tsp.	(5 ml)	vanilla extract
1 cup	(250 ml)	buttermilk or sour milk (see page 26)
2 tbsp.	(30 ml)	liquid red food color (one 1 oz./28 ml bottle)
2 cups	(500 ml)	all-purpose flour
⅓ cup	(75 ml)	unsweetened cocoa powder
1½ tsp.	(7 ml)	baking soda
1 tbsp.	(15 ml)	white vinegar

Preheat the oven to 350°F (180°C). Line two 9-inch (23 cm) round cake pans or one 9 x 13-inch (23 x 33 cm) rectangular cake pan with parchment paper. Grease the paper and the sides of the pan.

In a large bowl, beat together the sugar, oil and eggs with an electric mixer until fluffy, 3 to 5 minutes. Beat in the vanilla.

In another bowl, stir together the buttermilk or sour milk with the red food color. In a third bowl, mix the flour, cocoa, salt and baking soda.

Add the buttermilk mixture to the egg mixture alternately with the flour mixture, in 2 or 3 additions, beating after each addition. Stir in the vinegar, just until mixed. Pour the batter into the prepared pans (if using two, make sure you divide the batter equally). Place in the oven and bake for 30 to 35 minutes, or until a toothpick poked into the middle of a cake comes out clean. Let cool in the pans for 10 minutes, then run a knife around the sides of the cake to loosen it from the pan. Turn the layers out onto a rack. Peel off the paper and let cool completely before frosting.

A thing of beauty.

Makes two 8 or 9 inch (20 or 23 cm) round layers or one 9 x 13-inch (23 x 33 cm) rectangular cake.

How many servings in a cake?

Of course it's impossible to tell you exactly how many servings you'll get from any specific cake because that depends on the size of each slice, what kind of cake and who you're serving. But here's a rough guide — your mileage may vary.

8 or 9-inch (20 or 23 cm) double layer round cake:
8 to 12 servings

8 or 9-inch (20 or 23 cm) single layer square cake:
9 to 20 servings

9 x 13-inch (23 x 33 cm) single layer cake:
24 to 35 servings

10-inch (25 cm) tube or bundt cake:
12 to 16 servings

9 x 5-inch (23 x 13 cm) loaf cake:
10 to 12 servings

Chocolate Cake in a Mug

For emergency use only.

¼ cup	(60 ml)	all-purpose flour
¼ cup	(60 ml)	granulated sugar
3 tbsp.	(45 ml)	milk
3 tbsp.	(45 ml)	vegetable oil
2 tbsp.	(30 ml)	unsweetened cocoa powder
1		egg
½ tsp.	(2 ml)	vanilla extract

In a large coffee mug, stir together all the ingredients until smooth. Place in the microwave (no, really) and nuke on high power for 2½ to 3 minutes (check it after 2½ minutes). The cake will rise out of the mug as it bakes, but it won't overflow. Let cool for a few minutes, then turn out onto a plate or — sure, why not? — eat it directly from the mug. Ice cream is recommended, but not essential.

Makes 1 or 2 servings.

Sponge Roll Cake

Extremely impressive. Easy as anything.

¾ cup	(175 ml)	all-purpose flour
¾ tsp.	(3 ml)	baking powder
4		eggs
¾ cup	(175 ml)	granulated sugar
1 tsp.	(5 ml)	vanilla extract
		Your choice of filling (see below)
		Icing sugar for dusting

Preheat the oven to 400°F (200°C). Line a 10 x 15-inch (25 x 38 cm) jelly roll pan or cookie sheet with ½-inch (1 cm) sides with parchment paper. Grease the paper and sides of the pan.

In a small bowl, mix the flour and the baking powder. Set aside.

In a large mixing bowl, beat the eggs with an electric mixer until foamy. Add the sugar and vanilla, and continue beating until the mixture becomes very light and thick and has just about doubled in volume. This will take 5 to 7 minutes. Gently fold in the flour mixture (sprinke it over the surface and stir it into the egg mixture using a rubber spatula), taking care not to deflate the batter. When the flour is thoroughly mixed in, spread the batter evenly in the prepared pan (smooth out any bumps). Bake for 8 or 9 minutes, until the top is very lightly browned and the cake springs back when you touch it. Remove from the oven and let cool for 2 or 3 minutes in the pan.

Lay a clean dish towel or cloth on a flat surface and sprinkle it all over with icing sugar. Run a knife around the edges of the cake to loosen it from the pan and quickly (!) flip the cake out onto the sugared towel. Peel off the paper. *Ta-da*! With a serrated knife, trim off the crispy edges (and eat them — this is the baker's bonus). There. The hard bit is over.

Now fill it as you like and roll it up. Choose one of the following options.

Jam or jelly: Spread about 1 cup (250 ml) of your favorite jam onto the still-warm cake. Using the towel to help, carefully roll the cake up (starting with the long side) as tightly as possible without squishing it. Transfer to a tray or platter and let cool completely, wrapped in the towel. Just before serving, sprinkle liberally with icing sugar.

Whipped cream or buttercream frosting: While the cake is still warm, gently roll it into the towel (starting with the long side) and let it cool completely. It's important to roll the cake up while it's still warm because once it has cooled, it may become difficult to roll without cracking. And since you can't put icing or whipped cream on a warm cake, you have to let it cool completely before filling. When the cake has completely cooled, carefully unroll it, then spread it with plain or flavored whipped cream or creamy chocolate or vanilla frosting. Reroll it, as firmly as possible without squishing. Sprinkle with icing sugar before serving. Or cover the outside with more icing, if you like.

Before serving, trim off the ragged ends of the roll to make it look all nice and tidy. Eat the trimmings yourself.

Makes one 14-inch (36 cm) roll, or about 12 servings.

Chocolate variation

Reduce the flour in the recipe to ½ cup (125 ml) and add ¼ cup (60 ml) unsweetened cocoa powder. Sift to mix. Otherwise, prepare and fill as usual.

Make a Fancy Yule Log Cake!

Prepare the chocolate variation of the Sponge Roll Cake recipe. Let the unfilled cake cool, rolled in a towel (using the technique for filling with whipped cream or buttercream described in the recipe). Unroll and spread the cooled cake with Chocolate Buttercream Frosting (page 166) or Fudgy Sour Cream Frosting (page 169). Roll up the cake firmly (but don't squish), beginning with a long side of the cake.

With a sharp knife, trim the two ends of the roll on a slight diagonal just to remove the ragged edges. (Snack time!) Cover the outside of the "log" with additional chocolate frosting. Make lengthwise scratches in the frosting using a fork to create a realistic bark effect or knots or whatever. Festoon with chocolate leaves (see page 149), or leaf-shaped candies, or whatever other decorations you consider appropriate.

There. Is that awesome or what?

Angel Food Cake

What's with the ungreased pan?

Never grease the pan when making an Angel Food Cake. As the cake bakes, the batter needs to grip the sides of the pan in order to rise nice and high. The delicate batter doesn't have enough structure to hold itself up otherwise — so it needs a little help on the way. Don't we all?

If you follow this recipe exactly and give it your undivided attention, you'll be rewarded with a feather-light, perfectly fluffy cake. No multitasking allowed — you'll need to focus.

1 cup	(250 ml)	cake and pastry flour, sifted
1½ cups	(375 ml)	granulated sugar, divided
1½ cups	(375 ml)	egg whites (about 12 eggs)
1½ tsp.	(7 ml)	cream of tartar
1½ tsp.	(7 ml)	vanilla extract

Preheat the oven to 375°F (190°C). Have ready a 10-inch (25 cm) tube pan with a removable bottom, but don't grease the pan.

Sift the cake flour, then measure it. Add ¾ cup (175 ml) of the sugar (this is only half of the total amount of sugar) and sift the flour and sugar together twice. Set aside.

In a large mixing bowl, beat the egg whites with an electric mixer until just foamy. Add the cream of tartar and the vanilla, and continue beating until soft peaks form but they remain moist and glossy. Now, very gradually, add the remaining ¾ cup (175 ml) of the sugar, a couple of spoonfuls at a time. Beat after each addition, scraping the sides of the bowl to make sure the sugar is thoroughly incorporated. Continue beating until all the sugar has been added and the egg whites form stiff, glossy peaks when you lift the beater from the bowl.

Fold the flour mixture gradually into the meringue, in 3 or 4 additions, by sifting it over the beaten egg whites and then folding it in very gently with a wide rubber scraper. Repeat until all the flour mixture has been added and the batter is smooth but still fluffy (be careful not to deflate the meringue — this keeps the cake light and airy). Pour into the prepared tube pan.

Bake for 35 to 40 minutes, or until the cake is light brown and the top springs back when you touch it. Don't open the door midway through the baking time just to see how things are going. Remember — this cake can be moody and irritable, so do not aggravate it.

Remove the cake from the oven and immediately invert the pan onto the neck of a wine bottle (or other tall bottle) so that the pan is suspended upside down. Let the cake cool completely. To remove from the pan, turn the cake right-side-up and carefully run a knife around the sides and the tube to release it from the pan. Remove the sides, run the knife along the bottom to loosen that as well, then invert the cake onto a platter. The rest of the pan should come away easily.

Makes 1 angelically light cake that is impossibly delicious with strawberries and whipped cream.

Flourless Orange and Almond Torte

This wonderful, gluten-free cake is made with whole oranges, which gives it an intense orange flavor. Stunningly easy to put together and absolutely delicious.

3		medium seedless oranges (about 1 lb./454 g total)
6		eggs
1¼ cups	(300 ml)	granulated sugar
2⅓ cups	(550 ml)	ground almonds
1 tsp.	(5 ml)	baking powder

Place the oranges — whole, uncut and unpeeled — in a saucepan and add water to cover. Bring to a boil over medium heat, then reduce the heat to low, cover and let simmer for 2 hours. Yes, 2 hours. Drain and let cool, then chop the whole oranges as finely as possible by hand or, more easily, with a food processor. Don't puree — the mixture should have some texture.

Preheat the oven to 375°F (190°C). Line an 8-inch (20 cm) springform pan (or deep cake pan that has 3-inch (7 cm) high sides) with parchment paper. Grease the paper and the sides of the pan.

In a large bowl, combine the eggs and the sugar, and beat with an electric mixer for 2 or 3 minutes, until thick and creamy. Beat in the almonds and baking powder, then add the oranges and beat just until mixed. Pour batter into the prepared pan and bake for 55 to 60 minutes, until a toothpick poked into the middle of the cake comes out clean. Remove from the oven, but let the cake cool completely in the pan. When it has cooled to room temperature, remove from the pan and serve. A dollop of whipped cream with a few fresh berries is a very good idea.

Makes one 8-inch (20 cm) cake, 8 to 12 servings.

Practically Perfect Pound Cake

Pound cake. So plain, but so good. With ice cream or fruit. With chocolate sauce. It's even delicious straight from the freezer (yes, we know you've done that). Here's a basic pound cake recipe — with a few not-so-basic variations.

2 cups	(500 ml)	all-purpose flour
1 tsp.	(5 ml)	baking powder
1 cup	(250 ml)	granulated sugar
¾ cup	(175 ml)	butter, softened
3		eggs
2 tsp.	(10 ml)	vanilla extract
½ cup	(125 ml)	milk

Preheat the oven to 325°F (160°C). Grease a 9 x 5-inch (23 x 13 cm) loaf pan.

In a bowl, stir together the flour and the baking powder. Set aside.

In a large bowl, beat the sugar and the butter with an electric mixer until well blended. Add the eggs, 1 at a time, beating well after each egg. Continue beating the mixture for 2 or 3 minutes after all the eggs have been added. Beat in the vanilla, then add the flour mixture in 2 or 3 additions, alternately with the milk, beating until the batter is smooth. Dump into the prepared loaf pan. Bake for 70 to 75 minutes, until a toothpick poked into the center of the cake comes out clean.

Let cool in the pan for 10 minutes, then remove and let cool completely on a rack before having your way with it.

Makes 1 practically perfect pound cake, about 12 servings.

Variations

Chocolate Swirl Pound Cake

In a small microwave-safe bowl, place a 1 oz. (28 g) square of semisweet chocolate and 2 tbsp. (30 ml) milk. Microwave on high power in two or three 30-second bursts, stirring after each zap, until the chocolate is melted. (Be careful not to overheat the chocolate or it will scorch.) Stir until smooth. Divide the cake batter equally into

2 bowls. Beat the chocolate mixture into one bowl of batter — leave the other bowl of batter plain. Spoon the two batters alternately into the prepared loaf pan, then run a knife or spatula through the batter to swirl them together gently. Bake as usual.

Lemon or Orange Pound Cake
Omit the vanilla from the basic recipe. Add the grated zest from 1 lemon or 1 orange and 1 tbsp. (15 ml) lemon or orange juice to the batter when you add the flour and the milk. Bake as usual.

Poppy Seed Pound Cake
Add 2 tbsp. (30 ml) poppy seeds to either plain or lemon pound cake batter when you add the flour. Bake as usual.

Vanilla

Shy, but talented, poor old vanilla rarely gets the respect it deserves. I mean, vanilla ice cream is even white, for heaven's sake. As if it doesn't even deserve a color. No wonder it's not taken seriously.

The vanilla bean itself is the seedpod of a tropical orchid. This whole pod is slowly dried, during which time it turns dark brown and develops the characteristic vanilla flavor. You can find whole vanilla beans in many supermarkets or specialty food stores. These are used to flavor sugar or cooked desserts. For baking, vanilla is most often used in "extract" form — basically alcohol that has been infused with the flavor of the vanilla bean. Genuine vanilla extract is expensive. But worth it. If you're already baking from scratch, don't you want to use the real thing?

To make sure you're not buying imitation vanilla, look for the words *pure* or *real* on the label — the two items are usually near each other in the store and the bottles can look very similar.

Foolproof Chocolate Chip Banana Cake

Here's the perfect afterlife for those squishy black bananas you forgot about. And some people don't believe in reincarnation!

1½ cups	(375 ml)	mashed bananas (4 or 5 medium bananas)
1¼ cups	(300 ml)	granulated sugar
2		eggs
½ cup	(125 ml)	vegetable oil
1 tsp.	(5 ml)	vanilla extract
2 cups	(500 ml)	all-purpose flour
2½ tsp.	(12 ml)	baking powder
½ tsp.	(2 ml)	baking soda
1 cup	(250 ml)	semisweet chocolate chips

Preheat the oven to 350°F (180°C). Grease a 9 x 13-inch (23 x 33 cm) rectangular baking pan.

In a large bowl, beat together mashed bananas, sugar, eggs, oil and vanilla.

In another bowl, stir together the flour, baking powder and baking soda. Add flour mixture to banana mixture and beat until smooth, then add in the chocolate chips. Dump batter into the prepared baking pan and bake for 30 to 40 minutes, or until a toothpick poked into the middle of the cake comes out clean.

Let cool completely before frosting with (may I recommend) Fudgy Sour Cream Frosting (page 169), Cream Cheese Frosting (page 171) or Chocolate Ganache Glaze (page 171).

Makes one 9 x 13-inch (23 x 33 cm) cake.

Chipless variation

Just leave the chocolate chips out of the recipe for a plain banana version of this cake. Still excellent.

Whole Wheat Positive
You can substitute whole wheat flour for all or part of the all-purpose flour in this recipe. Start with a small proportion, and if you like the result, you can use more whole wheat flour next time.

Gluten-Free Friendly
Substitute gluten-free all-purpose flour for the regular all-purpose flour in this recipe. Results may differ slightly from the original version.

Anything Upside-Down Cake

For once, upside down is not an accident. Really — We meant to do that!

2 cups	(500 ml)	prepared fruit (see sidebar)
2 tbsp.	(30 ml)	butter, melted
½ cup	(125 ml)	brown sugar
1 tbsp.	(15 ml)	lemon juice
1 cup	(250 ml)	granulated sugar
2		eggs
½ cup	(125 ml)	milk
⅓ cup	(75 ml)	vegetable oil
1¼ cups	(300 ml)	all-purpose flour
1 tsp.	(5 ml)	baking powder
1 tsp.	(5 ml)	vanilla extract

Preheat the oven to 350° F (180° C). Grease an 8 or 9-inch (20 or 23 cm) round or square baking pan.

In a bowl, toss the prepared fruit with the melted butter, brown sugar and lemon juice until everything is evenly coated. Arrange the fruit on the bottom of the prepared pan in an artistic and decorative manner. Or just carelessly spread it out in a single layer. Whatever.

In a bowl, beat the granulated sugar and the eggs with an electric mixer until slightly thickened — about 1 minute. Add the milk, oil, flour, baking powder and vanilla, and beat for another minute — just until the batter is smooth and creamy. Pour the batter over the fruit in the baking pan and bake for 30 to 35 minutes, until very lightly browned.

When the cake has finished baking, remove it from the oven. Let the upside-down cake (which is still right-side-up at this point) cool in the pan for 5 minutes, then run a knife around the edges to loosen it. Hold a plate over the pan, and all at once flip the thing over. The upside-down cake should now be properly upside-down, with the artistically arranged fruit clearly visible. If any fruit clings to the baking pan, just scrape it off and rearrange it on the cake top. Serve warm with ice cream. Or plain.

Makes 6 to 8 servings.

Gluten-Free Friendly
Substitute gluten-free all-purpose flour for the regular all-purpose flour in this recipe. Results may differ slightly from the original version.

Pick a Fruit!

Any fruit. Well, almost any fruit. Pineapple is a classic, of course. But it's not the only fruit that you can use in this recipe. Here are some ideas:

Apples — peeled, cored and thinly sliced

Peaches — pitted, peeled and sliced

Pears — peeled, cored and thinly sliced

Blueberries — fresh or frozen

Bananas — peeled and thinly sliced

Pineapples — canned or fresh (peeled, cored and sliced)

Triple Chocolate Zucchini Cake

If you're drowning in a bumper crop of garden zucchini, this cake won't put much of a dent in the oversupply. Even so, it's definitely worth making. In fact, it's good enough that you might want to go out and buy a zuke if you don't happen to have one.

1 cup	(250 ml)	granulated sugar
¼ cup	(60 ml)	vegetable oil
2		eggs
1 tsp.	(5 ml)	vanilla extract
1¼ cups	(300 ml)	all-purpose flour
½ cup	(125 ml)	unsweetened cocoa powder
2 tsp.	(10 ml)	baking powder
1 cup	(250 ml)	shredded zucchini (one 6-inch/15 cm zuke)
½ cup	(125 ml)	semisweet chocolate chips
1 recipe		Chocolate Ganache Glaze (page 171)

Preheat the oven to 350°F (180°C). Grease an 8 or 9-inch (20 or 23 cm) square baking pan.

In a bowl, whisk together the sugar, oil, eggs and vanilla.

In another bowl, stir together the flour, cocoa powder and baking powder. Add the flour mixture to the egg mixture along with the shredded zucchini and stir until the batter is evenly combined. It will seem stiff and dry at first, but keep stirring and the zucchini will release enough liquid to help make the batter mixable. Stir in the chocolate chips. Spread batter in the prepared baking pan and bake for 35 to 40 minutes, until a toothpick poked into the middle of the cake comes out clean. Let cool completely before spreading Chocolate Ganache Glaze over the top of the cake. Chill just until glaze is set.

Makes one 8 or 9-inch (20 or 23 cm) square cake.

Fresh Apple Cake

Wouldn't a nice warm piece of freshly baked apple cake go well with that cup of coffee? Peeling the apples is the hardest part of making this quick cake. Which makes it pretty easy.

2 cups	(500 ml)	all-purpose flour
1 tbsp.	(15 ml)	baking powder
½ cup	(125 ml)	granulated sugar, divided
1 cup	(250 ml)	milk
1		egg
¼ cup	(60 ml)	vegetable oil
3		large apples, peeled and cored and thinly sliced
1 tsp.	(5 ml)	cinnamon
1 tbsp.	(15 ml)	butter

Preheat the oven to 425°F (220°C). Grease an 8 or 9-inch (20 or 23 cm) square baking pan.

In a large bowl, stir together the flour, baking powder and ¼ cup (60 ml) of the sugar (note — this is just half of the total amount of sugar). Set aside.

In another bowl, whisk together the milk, egg and vegetable oil. Add the milk mixture to the flour mixture all at once and stir just until combined. The batter will be slightly lumpy — this is fine. Spread the batter evenly in the prepared baking pan. Arrange the apple slices in overlapping rows (or zigzags or whatever) to completely cover the top of the cake.

In a small bowl, mix the remaining ¼ cup (60 ml) of sugar (remember?) with the cinnamon. Sprinkle this over the apples, then dot the top of the cake, here and there, with the butter. Bake for 25 to 30 minutes, until the apples are tender when poked with a fork, and the top is browned. Let cool slightly before cutting into squares. Serve warm or at room temperature.

Makes one 8 or 9-inch (20 or 23 cm) square cake.

Marble Bundt Cake

Here's a nice, basic marble cake that goes especially well with a cup of espresso or a tall glass of cold milk. It needs nothing more than a dusting of icing sugar to finish it off.

¾ cup	(175 ml)	butter, softened
1½ cups	(375 ml)	granulated sugar
3		eggs
1½ tsp.	(7 ml)	vanilla extract
¾ cup	(175 ml)	milk
2½ cups	(600 ml)	all-purpose flour
2 tsp.	(10 ml)	baking powder
½ cup	(125 ml)	chocolate syrup (the regular chocolate milk kind)
¼ tsp.	(1 ml)	baking soda
		icing sugar for dusting

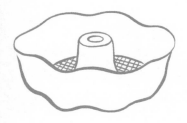

Preheat the oven to 325°F (160°C). Grease a 10-inch (25 cm) bundt pan very well, making sure you get into all the lumps and grooves.

In a large bowl, beat the butter, sugar, eggs and vanilla with an electric mixer, until very smooth and creamy — about 2 or 3 minutes. Add the milk, a little at a time, while you continue to beat the mixture for another minute or two. The mixture should be fluffy and smooth.

In another bowl, stir together the flour and baking powder. Add this to the butter mixture — in 3 or 4 portions — beating after each addition until everything is combined.

Pour about ⅔ of the batter into the prepared bundt pan. To the remaining batter in the bowl, add the chocolate syrup and the baking soda, and beat with mixer just until blended. Dollop the chocolate batter over the white batter and then, using a spatula or knife, gently swirl the two batters together — don't blend them into a mucky mixture — you want to retain the marbled effect. Bake for 60 to 75 minutes, or until a toothpick poked into the center of the cake comes out clean. Let cool in the pan for about 30 minutes, then loosen the sides gently with a knife and invert the cake onto a plate or cooling rack. Sprinkle lavishly with icing sugar just before serving.

Makes one 10-inch (25 cm) bundt cake.

Poppy Seed Yogurt Bundt Cake

Light, delicious and freckled with poppy seeds — perfect for teatime. Dust it with icing sugar or drizzle it with Shiny Sugar Glaze (page 173), or just leave it naked. It's all good.

1 cup	(250 ml)	plain yogurt
½ cup	(125 ml)	poppy seeds
1 cup	(250 ml)	granulated sugar
¾ cup	(175 ml)	vegetable oil
4		eggs
2 tsp.	(10 ml)	vanilla extract
2½ cups	(600 ml)	all-purpose flour
2 tsp.	(10 ml)	baking powder
1 tsp.	(5 ml)	baking soda

Preheat the oven to 325°F (160°C). Grease a 10-inch (25 cm) bundt pan very well, making sure you get into all the lumps and grooves.

In a small bowl, stir together the yogurt and the poppy seeds. Let soak while you gather the other ingredients and prepare the rest of the recipe.

In a large bowl, beat the sugar, oil, eggs and vanilla with an electric mixer for 2 or 3 minutes, until fluffy and thickened.

In another bowl, stir together the flour, baking powder and baking soda. Add the flour mixture to the egg mixture, in 2 or 3 additions, alternately with the poppy seed mixture. Beat until smooth after each addition. Pour batter into the prepared bundt pan and bake for 50 to 60 minutes, until cake passes the toothpick test (see page 23). Remove from the oven and let cool for about 10 minutes, then loosen the sides of the cake from the pan and invert it onto a plate or rack. Let cool completely.

To serve, sprinkle with icing sugar or drizzle with Shiny Sugar Glaze (page 173). Or serve it plain.

Makes one 10-inch (25 cm) bundt cake.

Overnight Buttermilk Coffee Cake

Yikes! It's your turn to do brunch! Mix up this coffee cake the night before and stash it in the refrigerator, unbaked. Pop it into the oven while you're taking your shower and it'll be ready before your guests arrive.

1 cup	(250 ml)	all-purpose flour
1 tsp.	(5 ml)	cinnamon, divided
½ tsp.	(2 ml)	baking powder
¼ tsp.	(1 ml)	baking soda
½ cup	(125 ml)	granulated sugar
⅓ cup	(75 ml)	butter, softened
½ cup	(125 ml)	brown sugar, divided
1		egg
½ cup	(125 ml)	buttermilk, thinned yogurt or sour milk (page 26)
¼ cup	(60 ml)	chopped walnuts or pecans

Grease an 8 or 9-inch (20 or 23 cm) square baking pan.

In a bowl, combine the flour, ½ tsp. (2 ml) of the cinnamon (this is just half of the total amount of cinnamon), baking powder and baking soda. Set aside.

In a large bowl, beat together the sugar, butter and ¼ cup (60 ml) of the brown sugar (only half the total amount) until fluffy. Add the egg and beat until smooth. Add the flour mixture in 2 or 3 additions, alternately with the buttermilk or other liquid, beating after each addition, until just smooth. Spread the batter in the prepared baking pan.

In a small bowl, stir together the remaining ½ tsp. (2 ml) of cinnamon, the remaining ¼ cup (60 ml) of brown sugar and the nuts. Sprinkle this mixture over the batter in the pan. Cover the pan with plastic wrap and refrigerate for several hours, or as long as overnight. (You can also bake it immediately, if you want.)

In the morning — or when you're ready to bake — preheat the oven to 350°F (180°C).

Remove the plastic wrap from the baking pan and bake the coffee cake for 40 to 45 mintues, or until a toothpick poked into the middle of the cake comes out clean.

Makes one 8 or 9-inch square cake.

There, now aren't you glad you made this last night?

Gluten-Free Friendly
Substitute gluten-free all-purpose flour for the regular all-purpose flour in this recipe. Results may differ slightly from the original version.

Blueberry Sour Cream Coffee Cake

Better than anything you can buy, this cake is absolutely delicious when still slightly warm.

2½ cups	(600 ml)	all-purpose flour
1½ tsp.	(7 ml)	baking powder
½ tsp.	(2 ml)	baking soda
¼ tsp.	(1 ml)	salt
1¼ cups	(300 ml)	granulated sugar
½ cup	(125 ml)	butter, softened
1½ tsp	(7 ml)	vanilla extract
2		eggs
1¼ cups	(300 ml)	sour cream or plain yogurt
2 cups	(500 ml)	blueberries, fresh or frozen (don't thaw)
1 recipe		All-Purpose Crumble Topping (page 182)

Preheat the oven to 350°F (180°C). Grease a 9 x 13-inch (23 x 33 cm) baking pan.

In a bowl, stir together the flour, baking powder, baking soda and salt.

In another bowl, beat the sugar, butter and vanilla with an electric mixer for 2 or 3 minutes, until blended and creamy. Add the eggs, one at a time, beating well after each egg. Now gradually add the flour mixture, alternately with the sour cream or yogurt, beating after each addition and scraping down the sides of the bowl often so that it all mixes evenly.

Set aside ½ cup (125 ml) of the blueberries and stir the remaining 1½ cups (375 ml) of blueberries into the batter. Dump batter into the prepared baking pan and spread evenly. Sprinkle the reserved blueberries over the batter, then sprinkle the top evenly with the Crumble Topping. Bake for 35 to 40 minutes, or until a toothpick poked into the middle of the cake comes out clean. Let cool for at least 30 minutes before serving.

Makes one 9 x 13-inch (23 x 33 cm) cake.

Flourless Chocolate Cake

Dense, fudgy and uncompromising — this is a cake for the truly committed chocolate lover. Plus, it's absolutely gluten-free. Cut small slices — it's powerful stuff.

2 cups	**(500 ml)**	**semisweet chocolate chips**
¾ cup	**(175 ml)**	**butter**
6 tbsp.	**(90 ml)**	**unsweetened cocoa powder**
10		**eggs, separated**
⅔ cup	**(150 ml)**	**granulated sugar**
		icing sugar, sweetened whipped cream and fresh berries for garnish

Preheat the oven to 350°F (180°C). Line the bottom of a 10-inch (25 cm) springform pan with parchment paper. Grease the paper and sides of the pan.

In a saucepan, over low heat, melt the chocolate chips and butter together, stirring until smooth. Remove saucepan from heat, add the cocoa powder and stir to blend completely. Set aside.

In a very large — scrupulously clean — mixing bowl, beat the egg whites with an electric mixer on high speed until foamy. Gradually add the sugar — a spoonful at a time — continuing to beat until stiff and glossy. Set this aside too.

In another large bowl, beat the egg yolks with the electric mixer for 3 to 5 minutes, until they just begin to thicken. Add the melted chocolate mixture and beat well. Stir about ¼ of the stiffly beaten egg whites into the chocolate mixture to lighten it, then very gently fold in the remaining egg whites, just until fairly well combined. Don't overmix the batter in an effort to eliminate all the streaks of white — it's better to leave a few streaks than to deflate the batter. Pour batter into the prepared baking pan. Bake for 40 to 45 minutes. The center of the cake will still be a bit soft. Fine.

Remove pan from the oven and let it cool for about 10 minutes. Loosen sides of cake by running a sharp knife around the edges, then invert cake onto a plate. Peel off the paper and let the cake cool completely. Refrigerate, covered loosely with plastic wrap, if you're not planning to serve it within a couple of hours. (You can bake this a day ahead of time, if you like — just keep it refrigerated until ready to serve.)

Just before serving, remove cake from the refrigerator and dust the top with icing sugar. Garnish each slice of cake with a glop of whipped cream and some fresh berries, if you have them. Be prepared to swoon.

Makes one 10-inch (25 cm) cake with 16 to 20 intensely chocolate servings.

Edible Chocolate Leaves: The Ultimate Cake Decoration

They're gorgeous, they're chocolate and they're easy to do. Guaranteed to make you famous.

You'll need:
- ✓ semisweet chocolate squares or bars (not chips)
- ✓ sturdy, nonpoisonous leaves — rose or lemon leaves are good (just be sure they haven't been sprayed with chemicals)
- ✓ waxed paper

First, line a baking sheet or tray with a sheet of waxed paper. Wash the leaves and make sure they're perfectly dry.

Now melt a few squares of semisweet chocolate (see chocolate melting instructions on page 95), stirring until smooth. Using a thin spatula or flat brush, apply a layer of chocolate to the underside of the leaves, almost (but not quite) all the way to the edges. Place the leaves, chocolate-side-up, on the waxed-paper-lined tray. Refrigerate for 10 minutes, until the chocolate has hardened. Working quickly, peel the leaf off the chocolate. Now you have a realistic, edible chocolate leaf that you can use to festoon your next cake. Keep the leaves refrigerated until you use them, and handle them as little as possible — the warmth of your hand will melt them.

There. Now, isn't that impressive?

Warm and Cozy Gingerbread Cake

It's a dark and stormy night. You need something warm and spicy to make you feel safe from monsters. This will do it.

1½ cups	(375 ml)	all-purpose flour
1 tbsp.	(15 ml)	ground ginger
1 tsp.	(5 ml)	cinnamon
½ tsp.	(2 ml)	baking soda
½ cup	(125 ml)	buttermilk, thinned yogurt or sour milk (page 26)
½ cup	(125 ml)	brown sugar
2		eggs
½ cup	(125 ml)	molasses
½ cup	(125 ml)	vegetable oil
		icing sugar for dusting, if desired

Preheat the oven to 350°F (180°C). Grease an 8 or 9-inch (20 or 23 cm) square baking pan.

In a bowl, stir together the flour, ginger, cinnamon and baking soda. Set aside.

In another bowl, beat the buttermilk (or whatever you're using), brown sugar, eggs, molasses and oil with a whisk or electric mixer until well blended. Add the flour mixture and beat the batter just until smooth. Pour into the prepared baking pan and bake for 30 to 35 minutes, until a toothpick poked into the middle of the cake comes out clean.

If you want to serve this warm (and why wouldn't you?), let the cake cool for about 10 minutes, then sprinkle the top with icing sugar and serve with whipped cream or ice cream. Or you can let it cool completely and frost with Cream Cheese Frosting (page 171) — also a very good idea.

Makes one 8 or 9-inch (20 or 23 cm) square cake.

Gluten-Free Friendly
Substitute gluten-free all-purpose flour for the regular all-purpose flour in this recipe. Results may differ slightly from the original version.

Classic Cheesecake

Everyone needs a good cheesecake recipe. This one is rich without being heavy, and lends itself to all sorts of excellent variations (which follow). It's the only cheesecake you'll ever need.

Filling

1½ lbs.	(750 g)	cream cheese, softened (three 8 oz./250 g packages)
4		eggs
2 tsp.	(10 ml)	vanilla extract
1 cup	(250 ml)	granulated sugar
1 recipe		crumb crust made with graham cracker or chocolate cookie crumbs (recipes on page 181)

Preheat the oven to 350°F (180°C). Grease the bottom and sides of a 10-inch (25 cm) springform pan.

Prepare the crumb crust mixture according to the recipe. Dump into the prepared springform pan, and press firmly and evenly onto the bottom (not up the sides) of the pan. Bake for 10 minutes. Let cool while you prepare the filling.

In a large bowl, beat the cream cheese with an electric mixer until smooth. Add the eggs, one at a time, beating well after each one. Add the vanilla and the sugar, beat well to mix, then pour into the prebaked crumb crust. Slam the pan down on the counter a couple of times to eliminate any bubbles. Bake for 45 to 50 minutes — the cake will still be quite moist in the middle, even a little wobbly. That's fine — it will set as it cools. Remove from the oven and let cool completely at room temperature.

When the cake is completely cool, you may find that the middle has sunk, but since you will probably cover the cake with a glaze or fruit topping, this is not a problem. Just ignore it. (You can also serve the cake plain, if you like. There's no law against that.)

Spread the topping of your choice (see page 153) evenly over the surface of the cake, or leave it plain if you prefer. Chill the cheesecake for several hours or overnight, before unlatching and removing the sides of the pan.

Makes one 10-inch (25 cm) cheesecake, 12 to 16 servings.

Don't forget to floss!

Your cake, that is.

Dental floss is the best thing to use to slice a cheesecake. Really. Here's how:

Just cut a lenth of floss wider than the diameter of your cake and hold one end in each hand. Press downward firmly, as if using a knife. The floss will cut right through the cake and give you perfect, straight slices with no gooey bits messing up the edges. Gorgeous.

Gluten-Free Friendly
Use gluten-free graham crackers to make the crust on this cheesecake.

Variations on a Cheesecake

Chocolate Swirl Cheesecake

Melt 2 squares (1 oz./28 g each) semisweet chocolate. Remove 2 cups (500 ml) of the prepared cheesecake filling mixture to a bowl and beat in the melted chocolate, mixing until blended. Dollop the chocolate mixture into the plain mixture and swirl it together, very gently, with a spatula or a wide bladed knife. (Better to leave it a little less mixed than to overblend it and lose the swirls.) Carefully turn this mixture into the pan, but try not to wreck the nice marbled effect. Bake as in basic recipe.

Raspberry Ripple Cheesecake

Into the prepared cheesecake filling mixture, spoon 1 cup (250 ml) canned raspberry pie filling, good raspberry jam or sweetened raspberry puree in large dollops. Swirl the raspberry goop through the plain cheesecake mixture very gently with a wide bladed knife or spatula. You want to create ripples of raspberry through the cake, so don't overmix it. Turn this mixture into the crust-lined pan, being careful not to mess up the swirls. Bake as in basic recipe.

Irish Cream Cheesecake

This is easy. Omit the vanilla from the basic recipe and instead add ⅓ cup (75 ml) Irish Cream liqueur. Bake as in basic recipe.

Beating Egg Whites

Seems impossible, doesn't it? That gloppy, gluey egg whites should turn into such lovely, puffy meringue? Well, it's not impossible — it's not even difficult.

Let your separated egg whites (see page 87 to learn how) come to room temperature in a large, fastidiously clean bowl. (Cold eggs are easier to separate, but room temperature eggs beat up fluffier.) Using an electric mixer on high speed, beat the egg whites until foamy, scraping down the sides of the bowl a few times with a rubber scraper. If your recipe calls for sugar to be added to the egg whites, you really have to add it gradually — a few spoonfuls at a time. This allows the sugar to slowly dissolve and be absorbed by the egg whites. Continue beating constantly at high speed until the egg whites are thick and white and glossy.

Most recipes will usually tell you to beat egg whites until they form stiff, glossy peaks. To know if you've reached this stage, stop beating and lift the beaters from the bowl. If the meringue stands upright in a shiny peak without collapsing, it's done.

A meringue made with sugar will be sturdier than egg whites beaten without any sugar added. In either case, be careful not to overbeat, because that will cause the meringue to collapse into a pathetic, useless mess. Better to underbeat than overbeat, I say.

Over-the-top Toppings

Chocolate Ganache Glaze
Prepare glaze on page 171. While still warm, pour evenly over the surface of the baked cheesecake, spreading to cover the top evenly. Then leave it alone to chill in peace.

Fruit Topping
Spread 1 cup (250 ml) prepared pie filling — raspberry, strawberry, blueberry, peach — over the baked and cooled cheesecake. Chill.

Fresh Berry Topping
Arrange whole fresh berries (any kind — whatever is in season) over the entire surface of the baked and cooled cheesecake. Heat 1 cup (250 ml) strawberry or apple jelly just until it liquefies, then spoon over the berries to glaze them. Chill until set.

Sour Cream Topping
Stir together 1 cup (250 ml) sour cream, 2 tbsp. (30 ml) granulated sugar and 1 tsp. (5 ml) vanilla extract in a small bowl. Spread over top of the cheesecake as soon as it comes out of the oven. Return cheesecake to the oven and bake for an additional 10 minutes. Cool and chill.

Lemon Curd Topping
Prepare Tangy Lemon Curd Filling (see page 172), and while it's still slightly warm and spreadable, spread it over the top of the cheesecake. Cool and chill until set.

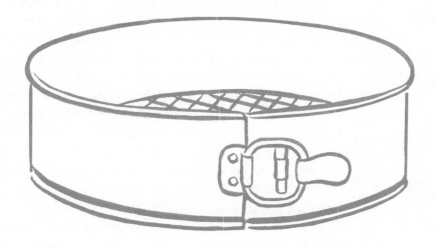

Molten Chocolate Lava Cakes

These seemingly harmless (ha!) little chocolate cakes erupt with molten chocolate lava when you poke your fork into them. Prepare the batter ahead of time and bake them just before you want to serve them — a diabolically delicious and crazy easy dessert.

5 squares		(1 oz./28 g each) semisweet chocolate
¼ cup	(60 ml)	butter
1 tbsp.	(15 ml)	brandy, rum or coffee liqueur
2		eggs
2		additional egg yolks
¼ cup	(60 ml)	granulated sugar
1 tsp.	(5 ml)	vanilla extract
1 tsp.	(5 ml)	instant coffee powder
1 tbsp.	(15 ml)	all-purpose flour
		whipped cream as an accompaniment

Grease four ¾ cup (175 ml) custard cups or miniature soufflé dishes.

In a small saucepan, melt together the chocolate and butter over low heat, stirring until smooth. Remove from heat and stir in the brandy (or whatever you're using). Let cool for a few minutes.

In a medium bowl, beat the eggs, additional egg yolks, sugar, vanilla and instant coffee powder with an electric mixer until quite thick — 3 to 5 minutes. When it's ready, the mixture will form a gloppy ribbon when you lift the beater from the bowl. Fold in the flour and the chocolate mixture, and mix just until combined.

Pour batter into the prepared baking dishes. Cover with plastic wrap and refrigerate until about an hour before you plan to serve dessert. The unbaked cakes can be prepared and refrigerated up to one full day ahead of time before baking.

Remove baking dishes from the refrigerator and let stand at room temperature for about 30 minutes to warm slightly.

Preheat the oven to 400°F (200°C).

Arrange baking dishes on a cookie sheet and bake for 11 to 12 minutes, until the cakes are set on the top but a toothpick poked into the center of one of the dishes comes out with batter clinging to it.

(These must be drastically underbaked in order to produce the crucial molten lava effect.) Let the cakes cool for 5 minutes, then carefully run a knife around the sides of each cake to loosen it from the dish; turn the cakes out onto individual serving plates.

Whipped cream is mandatory. Fresh berries are nice. Chocolate shavings are optional.

Makes 4 thoroughly evil servings.

Gluten-Free Friendly
Substitute gluten-free all-purpose flour for the regular all-purpose flour in this recipe. Results may differ slightly from the original version.

Whipped Cream — It's Always a Good Thing

Real honest-to-goodness whipped cream is never out of place. You can serve it with something as simple as a brownie to dress it up, or swirl some on top of a creamy cheesecake for the ultimate in too-muchness. Here's how to make it:

Plain Whipped Cream
Very lightly sweetened — it goes with everything.

1 cup	**(250 ml)**	**whipping cream (about 35% butterfat)**
2 tbsp.	**(30 ml)**	**granulated sugar**

First, make sure everything you'll be using — the bowl, the beaters and the cream — are very cold. It's helpful (but not absolutely necessary) to stash the bowl and beaters in the freezer for a few minutes before beating. Warmth is the enemy of whipped cream.

Combine the whipping cream with the sugar in the cold mixing bowl. Beat with an electric mixer on high speed, scraping down the sides of the bowl from time to time, until thickened. Stop beating as soon as the cream is thick enough to mound up when you drop it from a spoon. (Overbeating will cause the cream to separate and go all clumpy — eventually it will turn into butter. You don't want this to happen.)

There you are. Use it in any way you see fit.

Makes about 2 cups (500 ml) real whipped cream.

Chocolate Whipped Cream
Increase sugar to ¼ cup (60 ml) and add 2 tbsp. (30 ml) unsweetened cocoa powder to the basic mixture above.

Mocha Whipped Cream
Increase sugar to ¼ cup (60 ml) and add 2 tbsp. (30 ml) unsweetened cocoa powder and 1 tsp. (5 ml) instant coffee powder to the basic mixture above.

Strawberry or Raspberry Whipped Cream
Increase the sugar to ¼ cup (60 ml). Fold ½ cup (125 ml) unsweetened pureed strawberries or raspberries (frozen ones are just fine) into the basic whipped cream, then beat briefly just until combined.

European Hazelnut Torte

Let's say your cousin Zsa-Zsa from Budapest is coming for dinner. This is what she would expect for dessert. Nothing less. Lucky for you, it's easy.

Torte layers

4		eggs
¾ cup	(175 ml)	granulated sugar
1 cup	(250 ml)	whole hazelnuts, toasted, loose skin rubbed off (see page 119)
2 tbsp.	(30 ml)	all-purpose flour
2½ tsp.	(12 ml)	baking powder
¼ cup	(60 ml)	apricot or raspberry jam

Coffee Whipped Cream

1½ cups	(375 ml)	whipping cream
½ cup	(125 ml)	granulated sugar
2 tbsp.	(30 ml)	instant coffee powder
2 tsp.	(10 ml)	vanilla extract

Preheat the oven to 350°F (180°C). Line two 8-inch (20 cm) round cake pans with parchment paper and grease the paper and sides of the pans.

In a blender (preferably), or in a food processor, combine the eggs and sugar. Blend on high speed until smooth and creamy. Now add the hazelnuts — yes, whole — put the lid back on the container and blend, scraping down the sides of the container once or twice, until the nuts are very finely ground and the mixture is smooth. Now add the flour and the baking powder, and blend just until combined.

Pour the batter evenly into the prepared cake pans. Bake for 18 to 20 minutes, or until very lightly browned. When the cake layers are done, they'll spring back when you touch the top lightly. Let cool for about 5 minutes, then loosen the sides of the cake from the pans by running a knife around the edges and invert onto a rack. Peel off the paper and let the layers cool completely.

When the layers are cool, prepare the Coffee Whipped Cream (page 55). Combine the whipping cream, sugar, instant coffee and vanilla in a bowl, and beat with an electric mixer until the cream is thick and forms stiff peaks when you lift the beaters from the bowl.

When you are ready to assemble the cake, place one layer on a serving plate and spread with jam. Place the second cake layer over it. Cover the top and sides evenly with the Coffee Whipped Cream, and garnish tastefully in a sophisticated European manner. That means no plastic spacemen.

Well, okay, just one spaceman. But no Lego guys.

Makes 1 perfect 8-inch (20 cm) torte, 8 to 12 servings.

Gluten-Free Friendly
Substitute gluten-free all-purpose flour for the regular all-purpose flour in this recipe. Results may differ slightly from the original version.

Smashed Caramel Garnish

You won't believe how cool this looks on a cake.

Measure 1 cup (250 ml) of sugar into a small, heavy-bottomed saucepan. Place over low heat and cook, without stirring, until the sugar begins to melt and caramelize. Continue to cook, stirring once in a while, until sugar is completely melted and golden. Remove from heat (immediately — you don't want it to burn) and pour onto a greased cookie sheet, then spread it into a thin, even layer. Let cool until hardened and brittle, about 10 minutes.

Pry the sheet of hardened sugar off the baking sheet and crack it into uneven shards. Make some big ones, some smaller ones, some pointy ones. Arrange these pieces, standing up randomly, in the icing on your cake. Anything too small to use as a decoration can be eaten by you. You deserve it.

There. Smashing, isn't it?

Lethal Chocolate Cupcakes

A cupcake. Simple. Innocent. Harmless. Right? Wrong. You've been warned.

1½ cups	(375 ml)	all-purpose flour
¾ cup	(175 ml)	granulated sugar
¼ cup	(60 ml)	unsweetened cocoa powder
1 tsp.	(5 ml)	baking soda
1 cup	(250 ml)	milk
¼ cup	(60 ml)	vegetable oil
1 tbsp.	(15 ml)	white vinegar
1 tsp.	(5 ml)	vanilla extract

Preheat the oven to 375°F (190°C). Line a 12-cup muffin pan with paper liners.

In a large bowl, stir together the flour, sugar, cocoa powder and baking soda. Add milk, oil, vinegar and vanilla. Beat with a whisk or electric mixer just until smooth.

Spoon batter into the prepared pan, filling the cups about ¾ full. Bake for 18 to 20 minutes, until a toothpick inserted into the center of a cupcake comes out clean. Remove cupcakes from pan and let cool completely on a rack before frosting, glazing or decorating to your heart's content. See opposite page for suggestions.

Makes 12 perfectly lethal cupcakes.

Gluten-Free Friendly
Substitute gluten-free all-purpose flour for the regular all-purpose flour in this recipe. Results may differ slightly from the original version.

Cupcake Creativity

A well-dressed cupcake is a perfect little work of art. The following are just a few ideas to get you started — beyond this, you're on your own.

- ✓ Dip each cooled cupcake into a bowl of warm Chocolate Ganache Glaze (see page 171) just to give the tops a shiny chocolate coating. You can add sprinkles at this point, if you insist. Let cool until the glaze is set.
- ✓ Spread the the tops of cooled cupcakes with a swirl of Cream Cheese Frosting (see page 171). Sprinkle with chopped nuts or shredded coconut.
- ✓ Cover cooled cupcakes with Fudgy Sour Cream Frosting (see page 169). Decorate with colorful candy polka dots or some kind of chocolate silliness (see page 170).
- ✓ Frost cooled cupcakes with Chocolate or Vanilla Buttercream Frosting (see pages 166–167). Top each one with a fresh strawberry or raspberry.
- ✓ Spoon plain or flavored whipped cream (see page 155) on each cupcake and top with fresh berries or sprinkle with chocolate shavings.

Horrible Holiday Fruitcake

This is a fruitcake for people who don't really like fruitcake. Light and fruity, not dark and heavy, with a buttery pound cake base. Actually pretty unhorrible.

2 cups	(500 ml)	all-purpose flour
2 tsp.	(10 ml)	baking powder
2 cups	(500 ml)	coarsely chopped pecans or walnuts
½ cup	(125 ml)	golden raisins
¼ cup	(60 ml)	candied pineapple, chopped
¼ cup	(60 ml)	red candied cherries, halved
¼ cup	(60 ml)	green candied cherries, halved
1 cup	(250 ml)	butter
1¼ cups	(300 ml)	granulated sugar
3		eggs
2 tbsp.	(30 ml)	orange juice
2 tsp.	(10 ml)	grated orange or lemon zest
2 tsp.	(10 ml)	vanilla extract
		brandy or liqueur for brushing, optional

Preheat the oven to 325°F (160°C). Grease two 9 x 5-inch (23 x 13 cm) loaf pans.

In a bowl, stir together the flour and the baking powder until evenly mixed.

In another bowl, mix the nuts, raisins, pineapple and cherries. Remove 2 tbsp. (30 ml) of the flour mixture and toss with the fruit until everything is evenly coated. Set both the fruit mixture and the flour mixture aside.

In a large bowl, beat together the butter and sugar with an electric mixer until creamy — this will take 3 to 5 minutes. Or so. Add the eggs, one at a time, beating well after each one. Then add the flour mixture, in 2 or 3 portions, alternately with the orange juice and beating well after each addition. Finally, stir in the fruit mixture, the orange or lemon zest and the vanilla, and mix just until everything is evenly combined. The batter will be quite thick, but that's okay. Spoon batter into the prepared loaf pans. Bake 60 to 70 minutes, until the top is browned and a toothpick poked into the center of a cake comes out clean.

Let cakes cool for 30 minutes in the pans, then remove and let cool completely on a rack. At this point you can brush the tops and sides with brandy (or whatever liqueur you like) to add a little snazz, or just leave the loaves naked. Either way, wrap tightly in foil and let the cakes age for a day or two before serving, to allow the flavors to blend.

Makes 2 horrible fruitcakes that are not very horrible at all.

Ack! Disaster!

Your cake fell out of the pan, upside down, onto the kitchen floor. Or the dog got it. Or it burned. Do you have to throw it away? Maybe. Maybe not.

Broken cake

You tried to get the cake out of the pan, but half of it stayed behind in the pan. Don't panic. It's nothing a little icing won't fix. Reassemble the pieces of cake on the serving plate and cover the whole business with an extra-thick layer of frosting, taking care to hide the seams and any bumpy parts. There. No one need ever know the truth.

Even more broken cake

Too broken to reassemble? Make trifle. You can use any kind of cake as a base for trifle. Even chocolate. Everyone will love it, and no one will ever suspect it's not what you had planned. See trifle recipe on page 163.

Completely disintegrated cake

We don't want to know how it happened. Never mind — you can make crumbs. Just put whatever's left of the cake into a food processor and pulse until the cake is coarsely chopped. Dump the bits out onto a baking sheet and bake at 300°F (150°C) for 10 to 20 minutes, or until crunchy and toasted. Store in a plastic container and sprinkle on ice cream or yogurt.

Dog got it

No, really — this you have to throw out.

Eek. It burned!

As soon as you discover that your cake has burned, remove it from the pan and trim away all the burned parts with a sharp knife. It's important to work quickly, because the burned taste can infiltrate the rest of the cake. If the unburned part tastes okay, just cover the whole thing with frosting and pretend it never happened.

It fell into the toilet. It was an accident — honest.

See "Dog got it" above. And be more careful next time.

Magical Lemon Pudding Cake

This seemingly simple dessert is, in fact, a highly complicated scientific wonder. Fluffy cake on top, delicious lemon sauce on the bottom — and it happens all in the privacy of your very own oven. Imagine.

2		lemons, zest grated, juice squeezed
¼ cup	(60 ml)	all-purpose flour
¼ tsp	(1 ml)	salt
¾ cup	(175 ml)	granulated sugar, divided
3		eggs, separated
1¾ cups	(425 ml)	milk
		whipped cream and fresh berries for serving

Preheat the oven to 350°F (180°C). Grease a 6-cup (1.5 liter) shallow baking dish (a soufflé dish or an 8-inch (20 cm) square baking pan will do). Set this baking dish into a larger pan filled with very hot water.

Measure out ⅓ cup (75 ml) of the lemon juice and set aside. (Reserve the rest of the juice, if there is any, for another use.)

In a large bowl, stir together the flour, ½ cup (125 ml) of the sugar and the salt. In another bowl, whisk together the egg yolks, milk, lemon zest and the ⅓ cup (75 ml) lemon juice. Add the egg yolk mixture to the flour mixture and whisk just until mixed.

Beat the egg whites in a large bowl with an electric mixer until foamy. Add the remaining ¼ cup (60 ml) of the sugar, one spoonful at a time, beating until it forms stiff, glossy peaks. Stir about ¼ of the beaten egg whites into the batter, and mix just until the whites are incorporated and the batter is lightened. Now gently fold in the rest of the egg white until mixed — be careful not to entirely deflate the mixture. The batter will be pretty runny — that's okay. Pour into the prepared baking dish (which is sitting in the water bath). Place in the oven and bake for 45 to 50 minutes, until puffy and lightly browned on top. Let cool for at least 15 minutes before serving with whipped cream and fresh berries. Serve warm or chilled — it's excellent either way.

Makes 4 to 6 servings.

Gluten-Free Friendly
Substitute gluten-free all-purpose flour for the regular all-purpose flour in this recipe. Results may differ slightly from the original version.

Accidental Trifle

Oops. You didn't mean to drop half the cake on the floor. Now what? Well, pick up the pieces, fish out the dirt and make a lovely trifle.

1		stale, broken or otherwise ruined plain cake
6 cups	(1.5 liters)	strawberries, raspberries, blueberries, peaches, bananas (or a combination) cut into bite-size pieces
1/3 cup	(75 ml)	granulated sugar, divided
1 recipe		vanilla custard from Vanilla Cream Pie recipe (page 192) or 2½ cups (600 ml) of a vanilla pudding mix
2 cups	(500 ml)	whipping cream
1/4 cup	(60 ml)	sherry, rum, fruit liqueur or fruit juice
1 cup	(250 ml)	strawberry, raspberry or apricot jam

Have ready a large deep bowl, preferably glass (so you can see all the layers) approximately 9 to 10-inches (20 to 25 cm) in diameter.

Cut the cake up into slices – ragged or messy is fine.

Prepare the fruit (wash, slice, peel – do whatever must be done) and toss it with 1/4 cup (60 ml) of the sugar. Set aside.

Prepare the vanilla custard and let it cool.

Beat the whipping cream with the remaining sugar – about 1 tbsp. (15 ml) – with an electric mixer until it is thick and holds a soft peak when you lift the beaters from the bowl.

Okay – now you can put it all together. Start with cake. Arrange about half the cake slices in the bottom of the bowl. Sprinkle with half the liqueur or fruit juice and spread with half of the jam. Top this with half of the fruit, dollop with half of the vanilla custard and spread with half of the whipped cream.

Now repeat – the rest of the cake, liqueur, jam, fruit, custard and, finally, whipped cream. Decorate the top of the trifle with a few extra berries or whatever you happen to have around.

There you go. No one will ever suspect it was an accident.

Makes 8 to 10 servings.

Cake-Building Ideas

Start with a basic cake (or two, add some frosting, a glaze, maybe some fruit or whipped cream. What have you got? Well, all kinds of things. Here are some ideas for creating your own original cake masterpieces. All the cake and frosting recipes are in this book.

Sacher Torte
You'll need one chocolate cake layer, sliced horizontally into two thin layers
Bottom layer: one half-thickness chocolate cake layer
Spread with: apricot jam
Cover with: one half-thickness chocolate cake layer
Top with: Chocolate Ganache Glaze

Black Forest Cake
You'll need two chocolate cake layers
Bottom layer: one chocolate cake layer
Spread with: prepared cherry pie filling (canned is fine)
Spread with: whipped cream
Cover with: one chocolate cake layer
Frost with: whipped cream
Decorate with: maraschino cherries and chocolate curls

Ice Cream Cake
You'll need one chocolate or yellow cake layer, sliced horizontally into two thin layers
In a deep springform pan, assemble as follows:
Bottom layer: one half-thickness cake layer
Fill with: two quarts (2 liters) ice cream, any flavor, softened
Cover with: one half-thickness cake layer and press down firmly
Place springform pan in the freezer until cake is frozen solid. Remove cake from springform pan, place on a serving plate and cover the entire outsides with whipped cream. Return to freezer until ready to serve.

Deep Dark Devil's Food Cake
You'll need two chocolate cake layers
Bottom layer: one chocolate layer
Spread with: Fudgy Sour Cream Chocolate Frosting or Chocolate Buttercream Frosting
Cover with: one chocolate layer
Frost with: Fudgy Sour Cream Chocolate Frosting or Chocolate Buttercream Frosting

Multistriped Cake

You'll need one layer each chocolate cake and yellow cake, each one sliced horizontally into two thin layers (so four thin layers total).

Bottom layer: one half-thickness yellow cake layer

Spread with: Vanilla Buttercream Frosting

Cover with: one half-thickness chocolate cake layer

Spread with: Chocolate Buttercream Frosting

Cover with: one half-thickness yellow cake layer

Spread with: Vanilla Buttercream Frosting

Cover with: one half-thickness chocolate cake layer

Frost with: Chocolate Buttercream Frosting

Strawberry (or Peach, or Blueberry, or Raspberry) Shortcake

You'll need two yellow cake layers

Bottom layer: one yellow cake layer

Fill with: sliced, sweetened berries or peaches

Spread with: whipped cream

Cover with: one yellow cake layer

Frost with: whipped cream

Decorate with: whole berries or peach slices

Boston Cream Pie

You'll need two yellow cake layers

Bottom layer: one yellow cake layer

Fill with: Vanilla Custard (see Vanilla Cream Pie recipe)

Cover with: one yellow cake layer

Frost with: Chocolate Ganache Glaze

Luscious Lemon Cake

You'll need two yellow cake layers.

Bottom layer: one yellow cake layer

Spread with: Tangy Lemon Curd Filling

Cover with: one lemon cake layer

Frost with: whipped cream

Decorate with: fresh pansies!

Frostings, Fillings and Frivolities

Chocolate Buttercream Frosting

This quick and easy chocolate frosting whips up in no time. Spread it on any cake you happen to have available. If you have any frosting left over, freeze it to use at another time.

½ cup	(125 ml)	butter, softened
4 cups	(1 liter)	icing sugar
½ cup	(125 ml)	unsweetened cocoa powder
1 tsp.	(5 ml)	vanilla extract
½ cup	(125 ml)	milk or cream

In a large bowl, beat the butter with an electric mixer, until creamy. Add the icing sugar, cocoa, vanilla and ¼ cup (60 ml) of the milk or cream, and beat until the mixture begins to clump up — it will still be quite dry. Add the remaining milk or cream and continue beating until the frosting is creamy, fluffy and absolutely perfect.

    Makes about 3 cups (750 ml) of frosting— enough to fill and frost a two-layer 8 or 9-inch (20 or 23 cm) round cake, the tops of two 8 or 9-inch (20 or 23 cm) square cakes, or the top of one 9 x 13-inch (23 x 33 cm) rectangular cake.

Beyond Chocolate

Start with basic Chocolate Buttercream Frosting and keep going.

Mocha Buttercream
Dissolve 1 tbsp. (15 ml) instant coffee powder or instant espresso powder in the milk or cream before adding it.

Mint Chocolate Buttercream
Add 1 tsp. (5 ml) peppermint extract to the basic recipe.

Nutella Buttercream
Add ½ cup (125 ml) Nutella spread to the basic recipe.

Chocolate Peanut Butter Buttercream
Add ½ cup (125 ml) smooth peanut butter to the basic recipe.

The Clueless Baker

Vanilla Buttercream Frosting

Got a cupcake craving? Here's the perfect frosting to put on top. And don't forget to lick the beaters — it's pretty much mandatory.

½ cup	125 ml	butter, softened
3 cups	750 ml	icing sugar
2 tsp.	10 ml	vanilla extract
½ cup	125 ml	milk or cream

In a large bowl, beat the butter with an electric mixer until creamy. Add the icing sugar, vanilla and ¼ cup (60 ml) of the milk or cream, and beat until the mixture begins to clump up — it will still be quite dry. Add the remaining milk or cream and continue beating until the frosting is smooth and creamy.

Makes about 2½ cups (625 ml) — enough to fill and frost a two-layer 8 or 9-inch (20 or 23 cm) round cake, the tops of two 8 or 9-inch (20 or 23 cm) square cakes, or the top of one 9 x 13-inch (23 x 33 cm) rectangular cake.

Vanilla Buttercream Gone Wild

Start with basic Vanilla Buttercream Frosting. Go crazy.

Coffee Buttercream
Dissolve 2 tbsp. (30 ml) instant coffee powder or instant espresso powder in the milk or cream before adding it.

Lemon Buttercream
Omit the vanilla from the recipe. Reduce the milk or cream to 6 tbsp. (90 ml). Add 2 tbsp. (30 ml) lemon juice and 1 tsp. (5 ml) finely grated lemon zest.

Orange Buttercream
Omit the vanilla from the recipe. Reduce the milk or cream to 6 tbsp. (90 ml). Add 2 tbsp. (30 ml) orange juice and 1 tsp. (5 ml) finely grated orange zest.

Coconut Buttercream
Use canned coconut milk instead of milk or cream in the recipe. Beat in ½ cup (125 ml) finely shredded coconut.

Cinnamon Buttercream
Add 1 tsp. (5 ml) cinnamon to the basic recipe.

White Chocolate Buttercream Frosting

Oh my. This is delicious.

5 squares		**(1 oz./28 g each) good-quality white chocolate**
½ cup	**(125 ml)**	**butter**
1½ cups	**(375 ml)**	**icing sugar**
1 tsp.	**(5 ml)**	**vanilla extract**

In a double boiler, or in a saucepan set over a pan of hot (not boiling) water, melt the white chocolate, stirring until smooth. (White chocolate scorches easily, so don't put it directly over a burner to melt.) Remove from heat and transfer to a mixing bowl.

Add the butter, icing sugar and vanilla, and beat with an electric mixer until creamy and smooth. If the icing is too thick, you can add up to ¼ cup (60 ml) milk, a few drops at a time, until the frosting is spreadable and perfect.

Makes about 2 cups (500 ml) — enough to frost the top and sides of an 8 or 9-inch (20 or 23 cm) square or round cake, or a rectangular 9 x 13-inch (23 x 33 cm) cake.

Fudgy Sour Cream Frosting

I know what you're thinking. You're thinking, Ick. Sour cream? Well, prepare to be amazed. This might just be the best and easiest chocolate frosting you'll ever make. Try it on your next pan of brownies.

2 cups	(500 ml)	semisweet chocolate chips
1½ cups	(375 ml)	sour cream
1 tsp.	(5 ml)	vanilla extract

In a double boiler, or in a saucepan set over a pan of hot (not boiling) water, melt the chocolate chips, stirring until smooth. Transfer to a mixing bowl.

Add the sour cream and the vanilla, and beat with an electric mixer until smooth and creamy. Let cool just until the frosting begins to thicken, but don't wait too long because it will quickly thicken beyond spreadability, forcing you to resort to Plan B (see sidebar). Spread frosting, while still soft, evenly over cake or brownies, then chill until set.

Makes enough to fill and frost one 8 or 9-inch (20 or 23 cm) two-layer cake, the top of one 9 x 13-inch (23 x 33 cm) cake or a couple of pans of brownies.

Plan B

The Fudgy Sour Cream Frosting cooled and it's too thick to spread. What now? Well, you can rescue it by heating it gently in a double boiler over simmering water, stirring just until it becomes spreadable again. Use immediately. And don't let it happen again.

Chocolate Silliness

When it comes to cake decorating, there are a million ways to be silly with chocolate. Here are just a few:

Drizzle it!

Melt semisweet chocolate in the usual way (see page 95) and pour it into a small plastic sandwich bag. Cut off one corner of the bag (a very small snip, please) and drizzle the melted chocolate over cookies, cakes or wherever you feel chocolate is necessary (it's none of our business). When you're done drizzling, simply throw the bag away and get on with life.

Squiggle it!

Make weird and wonderful chocolate cake decorations by drizzling crazy patterns and squiggles onto waxed paper. Let the chocolate harden, then peel off the squiggly shapes and use to festoon a cake or pie.

Scribble it!

Using the plastic bag technique above, write the birthday person's name in chocolate on waxed paper. Refrigerate until hardened, then peel it off the paper and use it to personalize a birthday cake. She'll be so impressed. (Special note: it is illegal to write rude things in chocolate. It just is.)

Shatter it!

Pour melted chocolate onto a waxed-paper-lined cookie sheet and spread it in a thin layer. Refrigerate until hard, then peel off the paper and break the chocolate into big shards. Use these to decorate a cake or pie in an extremely artistic (yet slightly menacing) manner. Very cool.

Curl it!

Warm a chunk of chocolate in your hand until the chocolate is slightly softened. Using a vegetable peeler, shave thin flakes of chocolate — they'll fall off in tubular curls. Don't handle the curls because they'll melt in your hand. Use a spoon to transfer them to wherever you're putting them.

Cream Cheese Frosting

A classic on carrot cake. Delicious elsewhere too.

4 cups	(1 liter)	icing sugar
1 cup	(250 ml)	cream cheese, softened
½ cup	(125 ml)	butter, softened
1 tsp.	(5 ml)	vanilla extract

In a medium bowl, beat together the icing sugar, cream cheese, butter and vanilla until fluffy and smooth.

Makes enough to fill and frost one 8 or 9-inch (20 or 23 cm) two-layer cake, the top of one 9 x 13-inch (23 x 33 cm) rectangular cake or the tops of two 8 or 9-inch (20 or 23 cm) square cakes.

Chocolate Ganache Glaze

This dark, rich chocolate glaze is strictly for the mature and serious chocolate lover. Glossy and smooth, not too sweet, dangerously delicious. It transforms an otherwise innocent cupcake into a public menace.

4 squares		(1 oz./28 g each) semisweet chocolate
¼ cup	(60 ml)	whipping cream
1 tbsp.	(15 ml)	butter

Roughly chop the chocolate into chunks and place in a small microwave-safe bowl. Add the whipping cream and microwave on high power for 30 seconds. Stir, then add the butter, microwave for another 20 seconds and stir until completely smooth. (You can also melt the chocolate and cream together in a small saucepan over low heat, if you prefer.) Let cool for 5 or 10 minutes before using.

Makes enough glaze for 12 cupcakes or one 8 or 9-inch (20 or 23 cm) round or square cake or pan of brownies. The recipe can be doubled if desired.

To glaze cupcakes:

Pour warm glaze into a small bowl. Holding each cupcake by the bottom, dip it into the chocolate glaze and twirl it so the glaze coats the top of the cupcake. Place on a tray and refrigerate, without disturbing, until the glaze sets.

To glaze a cake or a pan of brownies:

Pour glaze evenly over the top and spread, while still warm, to cover the surface evenly. Refrigerate until set. (Don't mess with the glaze once it's set or you'll ruin the effect.)

Tangy Lemon Curd Filling

Glaze a cheesecake, spoon onto freshly baked biscuits or spread between two cake layers — this is just too good to be so easy.

½ cup	(125 ml)	lemon juice
½ cup	(125 ml)	granulated sugar
1		egg
¼ cup	(60 ml)	butter

In a large microwave-safe bowl (at least 4 cups/1 liter), whisk together the lemon juice, sugar and egg. Add the butter, cut into chunks. Place in the microwave and nuke on high power for 1 minute. Open the door, whisk the mixture and continue to microwave in 30-second bursts, whisking after each one. Depending on the power of your microwave, the lemon curd may take between 4 and 6 minutes to thicken. It's done when it looks glossy and clear-ish and it begins to mound up a bit when you stir it. As soon as that happens, remove it from the microwave, mix well and transfer to a covered container. Refrigerate.

Makes about 1½ cups (375 ml) lemon curd.

Royal Decorator Icing

This icing dries hard and white — ideal for decorating gingerbread or sugar cookies.

1½ cups	(375 ml)	icing sugar
1		egg white
½ tsp.	(2 ml)	lemon juice

In a medium bowl, beat together the icing sugar, egg white and lemon juice until light and fluffy. The more you beat, the better the icing, so don't worry about overdoing it. You can divide the icing into several bowls and tint each bowl of icing a different color if you require a multicolored effect.

Keep the icing tightly covered with plastic wrap, to prevent it from drying out until you're ready to use it.

The Clueless Baker

Shiny Sugar Glaze

This sugar glaze is especially good on coffee cakes, bundt cakes and cookies. It dries to a very pretty, glossy finish.

1 cup	**(250 ml)**	**icing sugar**
2 tbsp.	**(30 ml)**	**water (or lemon juice)**

In a small bowl, stir together the icing sugar with the water or lemon juice — adding the liquid a little bit at a time, until smooth. Spread on cookies or drizzle over coffee cake — then leave it alone until it dries.

That's it.

Makes about 1 cup (250 ml).

Last-minute Desperate Cake-decorating Idea

Yikes! You made a cake, but you don't have time to make icing. The cake looks so naked sitting there on the plate. Don't panic. Just spoon some icing sugar into a small strainer and dust your cake until the top is evenly powdered. If you're feeling creative, you can place paper cutouts of stars or stripes or even a paper doily on top of the cake before dusting. Lift the stencil off carefully and voilà! A very impressive design. Hardly looks desperate at all.

Clueless Troubleshooting: Cakes and Frostings

The last thing you need from a cake is trouble. But — alas — it happens. Despite the trauma of the collapsed birthday cake or the cracked cheesecake, you will live to bake again. Here are some common problems and some ways to avoid a repeat performance of whatever disaster you just experienced:

It didn't rise at all.
✓ Did you forget to add the baking powder or baking soda? Are you sure?
✓ How old is your baking powder/soda? Is it the same package you bought when you moved into your house five years ago? Treat yourself to a fresh package — the stuff doesn't last forever.
✓ Did you let the batter sit around for a while before baking it? Baking soda and baking powder begin working as soon as the batter is mixed. If not baked right away, the batter may get tired and simply give up. Get it into the oven quickly next time.
✓ If the recipe called for separated eggs, did you beat the egg whites to the point of collapse? Next time, beat them only until they hold a peak when you lift the beater out of the meringue. Any longer and they may fall apart.
✓ Were you a little, er, overenthusiastic when you folded the beaten egg whites into the rest of the batter? They have to be treated gently so as not to deflate them. It's better to leave a few white streaks in the batter than to overmix the whole business.

It rose nicely, then collapsed.
✓ This can happen with a light cake like an angel food cake, because it's so delicate that there's not much structure to hold the whole thing up. Next time, be sure your egg whites are stiffly beaten (but not overbeaten — see above), measure all the ingredients carefully and be sure to sift the flour.
✓ Did you take it out of the oven before it was fully baked? Do the toothpick test next time (see page 23).
✓ Fluctuating oven temperature can annoy a baking cake, causing it to throw a snit and collapse.

Ack — it's all lopsided! The cake, I mean.

✓ Your oven may heat unevenly, causing some areas to be hotter than others. Rotate the pans in the oven midway through the baking time to help avoid lopsidedness. Turn them back to front, and switch oven racks. This may not totally cure the problem, but it could reduce it.

✓ Are your oven racks bent? Check them. If the batter is on a slant in the baking pan when you place it on the rack, your cake will turn out lopsided.

✓ Quick and dirty solution: If your cake will be covered with frosting, just slice off the lopsided bits to even the cake out. Who's going to know?

The bottom burned before the cake was done.

✓ If your oven heats unevenly, you can try moving your cake pans to a higher shelf next time. Or simply lower the heat by 10 to 25 degrees. Get an oven thermometer and use it. It can avoid a lot of aggravation.

The batter overflowed in the oven.

✓ Your pan was probably too small for the amount of batter. Check the volume of the baking pan, or measure the diameter to make sure you're using the correct pan for the recipe.

The dog ate my boyfriend's entire birthday cake! Now what?

✓ Is the bakery still open? Go there. Tell them we sent you.

The top (or bottom) of the cake is sticky.

✓ Cool your cake on a rack after removing it from the pan, to allow the air to circulate around it.

✓ Humid weather may cause a cake to absorb moisture and become sticky. Can't be helped.

My cheesecake cracked!

✓ You probably overbaked it. Reduce the baking time by several minutes next time you make it. The filling may not appear done, but it will continue to solidify as the cheesecake cools. And it will have a creamier texture too.

✓ But hey — you can fix it. Sort of. Covering the top of your cheesecake with a thick fruit glaze (canned fruit pie filling — such as blueberry or raspberry) will hide a multitude of evils. You can also spread the top of the cake with sweetened whipped cream, sour cream, lemon curd (page 153) or a lovely Chocolate Ganache Glaze (page 171).

Why am I doing this?!?!?

Five good reasons (and five so-so ones) to bake at home:

1. Baking is fun. Really, it is.

2. Anything home baked will taste a zillion times better than anything you can buy. Except maybe that chocolate croissant you once bought from a little pâtisserie in Paris (but possibly better than that, even).

3. You can be sure there will be no monophosphate disodium tetrachloride whatsoever in your coffee cake. Unless you put it there. And why would you?

4. Baking makes your kitchen smell wonderful.

5. It is a scientific fact that freshly baked homemade chocolate chip cookies are the single best thing on the planet.

6. You can impress and influence girlfriends/boyfriends/ husbands/wives/bosses/among others.

7. If it is your birthday and no one gets you a cake, you can make one for yourself!

8. It's a cool thing to do with little kids.

9. There are rat hairs in packaged cookies. Just kidding. (But how do you know there aren't?)

10. You can't get to lick the beaters if you haven't beaten anything.

Pies and Other Pastries

Pastry. The very word can strike terror in the hearts of otherwise brave and competent cooks. Nightmare memories of tough, inedible crusts, glutinous fluorescent fillings, creepy chemical flavors. Relax, it doesn't have to be that way.

Making a pie is not rocket science. In fact, it's easy as, well, pie. All you need is a reliable pastry recipe (or two), a few fabulous fillings and a little practice. It'll be fine — really it will.

Basic Pastry Recipes

Foolproof Plain Pastry

This recipe makes enough dough for five single pastry crusts. Mix up the whole batch — it's no more work than making a single crust — and freeze in individual-crust portions, tightly wrapped in plastic, for future baking.

4 cups	(1 liter)	all-purpose flour
1 tbsp.	(15 ml)	granulated sugar
½ tsp.	(2 ml)	salt
1¾ cups	(425 ml)	solid vegetable shortening, very cold (frozen, even)
½ cup	(125 ml)	water
1 tbsp.	(15 ml)	vinegar
1		egg

It's Better with Butter

Shortening makes pastry dough light and flaky, and it's easy to work with. But butter gives pastry a rich flavor and is a more natural ingredient. Once you've mastered this basic pastry recipe, try making it with half shortening and half butter. If you like how it turns out, you can increase the proportion of butter to see what gives you the best pastry. Experiment!

In a very large bowl, stir together the flour, sugar and salt. Cut the vegetable shortening into chunky pieces and add to the flour mixture in the bowl. Now, with a pastry blender or two knives (see page 179), cut the shortening into the flour mixture until it is very crumbly and resembles coarse oatmeal.

In a smaller bowl, beat together the water, vinegar and egg until blended. Stir into the flour mixture, tossing gently until everything is evenly dampened and can be gathered into a soft dough that sticks together. Don't stir and don't mash — you want the whole mess to stay lightly mixed.

With well-floured hands, divide the dough into 5 equal pieces. Pat them into flattish disks, flouring the outsides well. Wrap individually in plastic wrap and refrigerate for an hour or two before using, or freeze to use some other time.

Makes enough pastry for 5 individual 8 to 10-inch (20 to 25 cm) piecrusts.

Cutting in Your Shortening

Sounds like something a tailor might do to your new pants, right? Wrong. This, in fact, is a method of combining the shortening (fat) with the flour when you make pastry or biscuit dough, in such a way as to leave little fat nuggets dispersed throughout the dough rather than blended in.

Why do we do this? Well, if you've ever poked a fork into a nice flaky piecrust, you'll notice that it crumbles into layers rather than breaking evenly like a cookie. Each eensy piece of shortening creates a tiny layer in the pastry dough — which is exactly what you want. Tricky? Not at all.

So here's what you do. Dump your flour into a bowl and combine it with any other dry ingredients (sugar, salt, spices and so forth.). Cut the solid shortening (butter, margarine, lard, solid vegetable shortening) into chunks and add it to the flour. Now, using an official pastry blender (a special utensil with wires or blades designed for this very task), chop the shortening into the flour, making smaller and smaller pieces until the mix is basically just a crumbly mess. (You can also use a couple of knives to do the chopping if you don't have a pastry blender — it's just a bit more awkward.) When the mix is all crumbly, but before it turns mushy, stop chopping.

A food processor, if you have one, makes quick work of this task — but you do have to be careful not to overprocess the mixture.

Now all that's left to do is add the liquid and mix lightly, and you're ready to roll out the dough. See, that wasn't so hard, was it?

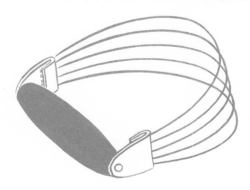

Rich Cream Cheese Pastry

This pastry can be used for piecrusts, tart shells or to make delicious rugelach (page 110).

2 cups	(500 ml)	all-purpose flour
1 cup	(250 ml)	butter
1 cup	(250 ml)	cream cheese (one 8 oz./250 g package)
2 tbsp.	(30 ml)	sugar

In a large mixing bowl, combine the flour, butter, cream cheese and sugar. With an electric mixer or by hand with a sturdy spoon, mix everything until it forms a uniform dough that can be handled. Divide the dough into 3 equal pieces and dust each piece lightly with flour. Pat the pieces of dough into flattish disks and wrap in plastic wrap. Refrigerate for at least 1 hour before using, or freeze to use another time.

Makes enough pastry for three 8 to 10-inch (20 to 25 cm) single piecrusts or 32 rugelach.

Flaky Sour Cream Pastry

This flaky pastry is perfect for making strudel (see page 202), turnovers or butter tarts (page 196). It rolls out beautifully and is very easy to work with.

1½ cups	(375 ml)	all-purpose flour
1 cup	(250 ml)	butter, very cold, cut into chunks
½ cup	(125 ml)	sour cream

In a large mixing bowl, combine the flour and the butter, cut into chunks. With a pastry blender or two knives, cut the butter into the flour until the mixture is very crumbly and resembles coarse meal (see page 179 for more elaborate details). Add the sour cream and stir just until a soft dough forms.

With well-floured hands, divide the dough into 2 equal pieces, dust each one lightly with flour so it's not sticky and pat into a flattish disk. Wrap in plastic wrap and refrigerate for an hour or two before using, or freeze to use another time.

Makes enough pastry for two 8 to 10-inch (20 to 25 cm) single piecrusts.

Basic Graham Cracker Crumb Crust

This basic recipe can be used to make a graham cracker pie shell or a crumb crust for cheesecake. Easy as, um, pie.

1½ cups	(375 ml)	graham cracker crumbs (about 18 crackers)
2 tbsp.	(30 ml)	granulated sugar or brown sugar
¼ cup	(60 ml)	butter, melted

Preheat the oven to 375°F (190°C).

Mix all the ingredients in a bowl until everything is evenly combined.

To make a pie shell, squish the mixture evenly into the bottom and up the sides of an 8 or 9-inch (20 or 23 cm) pie plate, pressing the crumbs firmly so that they stick. (A supereasy trick to do this: spread the crumb mixture into a pie plate and smush down with a second pie plate to evenly distribute the crumbs in a neat layer.)

For a cheesecake crust, dump the crumbs into the bottom of a springform pan and pat them down into an even layer. It's not necessary to have the crumbs climb up the sides of the pan.

Bake for 8 to 10 minutes, then let cool before filling

Makes one 8 to 10-inch (20 to 25 cm) pie shell, or a bottom crust for a 9 or 10-inch (23 or 25 cm) cheesecake.

Gluten-Free Friendly
Use gluten-free graham crackers or other gluten-free cookies to make the crumbs for this crust. Perfect anywhere you need a crumb crust.

Variation

Chocolate or Vanilla Crumb Crust
Use chocolate wafer crumbs or vanilla wafer crumbs instead of the graham cracker crumbs. (This works out to about 30 chocolate wafers or 36 vanilla wafers, crushed.) Follow basic recipe on this page.

All-Purpose Crumble Topping

A million uses! Top an apple pie — sprinkle over unbaked muffins or coffee cake — make a warm fruit crisp. Mix up a double batch and refrigerate, or freeze so it's ready to use whenever you need it.

1 cup	**(250 ml)**	**all-purpose flour**
½ cup	**(125 ml)**	**butter**
½ cup	**(125 ml)**	**brown sugar**
½ tsp.	**(2 ml)**	**cinnamon**

Combine the flour, butter, brown sugar and cinnamon in a large bowl (or in the bowl of a food processor). Smush the butter into the mixture until it forms a slightly sticky crumbly mixture. If you're using a food processor, quick on-off pulses will give you the best texture.

Sprinkle on whatever it is you're making and bake according to whatever recipe you're using. This recipe can easily be doubled so that it's always ready to use when you need it.

Makes enough to top one 8 to 10-inch (20 to 25 cm) pie or one pan of fruit crumble (see opposite page).

Whole Wheat Positive
You can substitute whole wheat flour for all or part of the all-purpose flour in this recipe. Start with a small proportion, and if you like the result, you can use more whole wheat flour next time.

Gluten-Free Friendly
Substitute gluten-free all-purpose flour for the regular all-purpose flour in this recipe. Results may differ slightly from the original version.

Any-Fruit Crumble

Pick a fruit, any fruit — fresh or frozen, they're all good. Use apples, peaches, rhubarb, strawberries, raspberries, blueberries, plums — or make up a mixture of whatever you have. Sprinkle with All-Purpose Crumble Topping, and ta-da! Almost instant dessert.

6 cups	**(1.5 liters)**	**prepared fruit (see sidebar)**
½ cup	**(125 ml)**	**granulated sugar**
3 tbsp.	**(45 ml)**	**cornstarch**
1 recipe		**All-Purpose Crumble Topping (page 182)**

Preheat the oven to 375°F (190°C). Grease an 8 or 9-inch (20 or 23 cm) square baking pan.

In a large bowl, toss the fruit with the sugar and cornstarch. You may want to adjust the amount of sugar to suit your taste and the sweetness of the fruit (rhubarb will need more sugar than ripe peaches). Dump into the prepared baking pan. Sprinkle the All-Purpose Crumble Topping evenly over the fruit in the baking pan. Bake for 35 to 45 minutes, or until the fruit bubbles around the edges of the pan and the topping is lightly browned. Let cool for a few minutes, then serve warm with ice cream or whipped cream.

Makes 6 to 8 servings.

That's the way the fruit crumbles

Apples, peaches, pears: peel, core (or pit) and cut into slices or chunks.

Plums, cherries: remove pits and cut into chunks, if necessary.

Berries: wash and remove stems, if necessary. Cut in half or leave whole.

Rhubarb: wash and cut into ½-inch (1 cm) pieces.

Pies and Other Pastries

Classic Double-Crust Fruit Pie

Start with pastry dough for an 8 to 10-inch (20 to 25 cm) double-crust pie (two single-pastry crusts). You can use any of the pastry recipes in this book (or cheat and buy prepared pastry). Roll out one crust for the shell, fill with your favorite fruit mixture (pick one!) and roll the second crust out to make a top crust. Don't panic — it's easy. Detailed instructions follow and helpful diagrams are on page 187.

Apple Pie

5 cups	(1.25 liters)	peeled, cored and thinly sliced apples
¾ cup	(175 ml)	granulated sugar
2 tbsp.	(30 ml)	all-purpose flour
1 tbsp.	(15 ml)	lemon juice
½ tsp.	(2 ml)	cinnamon
		Prepared pastry for a double-crust pie

Blueberry Pie

5 cups	(1.25 liters)	blueberries, fresh or frozen (if frozen, don't defrost)
¾ cup	(175 ml)	granulated sugar
¼ cup	(60 ml)	cornstarch
1 tbsp.	(15 ml)	lemon juice

Peach Pie

5 cups	(1.25 liters)	peeled, pitted and sliced peaches (if frozen, don't defrost)
¾ cup	(175 ml)	granulated sugar
2 tbsp.	(30 ml)	all-purpose flour

2 tbsp.	(30 ml)	cornstarch
1 tbsp.	(15 ml)	lemon juice

Rhubarb or Strawberry-Rhubarb Pie

5 cups	(1.25 liters)	chopped fresh or frozen rhubarb or half-and-half rhubarb and strawberries (if frozen, don't defrost)
1 cup	(250 ml)	granulated sugar
¼ cup	(60 ml)	cornstarch

Preheat oven to 375°F (190°C). Have ready a 9 or 10-inch (23 or 25 cm) pie pan.

Dust a table or other surface with flour, place one disk of pastry dough on this floured surface and dust the dough with flour. With a rolling pin, roll the dough out to a 12 to 14-inch (30 to 35 cm) circle, as evenly as possible. You may need to dust the dough with flour several times as you roll it, to keep it from sticking to the rolling pin or table. Carefully transfer the pastry to the pie pan — fold the pastry in half or quarters to make it easier to handle (see diagram on page 187). Unfold the dough carefully and position it in the pan so that it's centered. Press gently into place. There will be excess dough hanging over the edges of the pan. If you plan to put a top crust on the pie, trim off the overhanging pastry dough even with the edges of the pan. But if you're making a one-crust pie or if you will be topping the pie with crumbs instead of crust, don't trim anything. (I'll get to that in a minute.) Don't panic if you've torn a hole in the pastry; just patch it with a little bit of dough — no one needs to know about it since it will be under the fruit.

In a large bowl, toss together all the ingredients for the fruit filling of your choice. Dump into the prepared pastry shell and smush the fruit lightly to fill the shell to the edges; mound it up a little in the center.

For a traditional double-crust pie, roll out the second lump of pastry dough on a well-floured surface — just like the first time — to form a circle just slightly larger than the diameter of the pan. You will need some overhang to seal the edges. Carefully transfer the rolled-out pastry to cover the fruit. Make sure it's centered over the filling and gently tuck the top crust under the edges of the trimmed bottom crust, rotating the pie pan a little at a time as you go around. This is a bit like putting a fitted sheet on a bed.

Make mine crummy!

Instead of covering your fruit filling with a pastry crust, try a crumble topping instead. Roll out a bottom crust and fill as usual. Instead of the top crust, sprinkle the unbaked fruit filling with All-Purpose Crumble Topping (page 182). Bake as for a double-crust pie. Great if you're not a big piecrust fan. And less work too.

For a single-crust pie, just fold the overhanging pastry neatly under, all around the edges to make a tidy border. This outside rim will be thick — that's okay.

Either way, now comes the fun part. Firmly crimp the crust in a fancy-pants ruffly manner all around the outside rim to make a fluted (technical term) edge. (See diagram on page 187.) Or just press all around the rim with a fork — either way is fine. This crimping not only makes a pie look awesome, but it also seals the juicy filling inside so that it doesn't leak all over the bottom of your oven. Cut 3 or 4 slits in the top crust to act as steam vents.

Bake for 50 to 60 minutes, until the fruit is soft (poke a sharp knife into the fruit through one of the steam vents to check) and the crust is golden brown. Let cool slightly before serving with, of course, vanilla ice cream.

Makes one 9 or 10-inch (23 or 25 cm) pie, 6 to 10 servings.

Killer Pecan Pie

Almost too much. But you can handle it.

Variations

Chocolate Pecan Pie
Melt 4 squares
(1 oz./28 g each)
semisweet chocolate
with the butter in the
basic recipe. Bake as
usual. Act nonchalant,
if possible.

Maple Walnut Pie
Substitute pure maple
syrup for the corn syrup
in the basic recipe, and
use walnuts instead of
pecans. Seriously great.

1 cup	(250 ml)	golden corn syrup
⅔ cup	(150 ml)	granulated sugar
3		eggs
¼ cup	(60 ml)	butter, melted
1 tsp.	(5 ml)	vanilla extract
1 cup	(250 ml)	coarsely chopped pecans
1		unbaked 9 or 10-inch (23 or 25 cm) pie shell

Preheat the oven to 350°F (180°C). Have ready an unbaked pie shell in baking pan.

In a large bowl, beat the corn syrup, sugar, eggs, melted butter and vanilla with an electric mixer until slightly thickened — 2 or 3 minutes. Stir in the chopped pecans and pour the into the prepared pie shell. Place the pan on the lowest shelf of the oven and bake for 55 to 60 minutes, or until a knife poked into the center of the filling comes out clean.

Ridiculously easy for something so good, isn't it?

Makes one 9 or 10-inch (23 or 25 cm) pie, 6 to 10 servings.

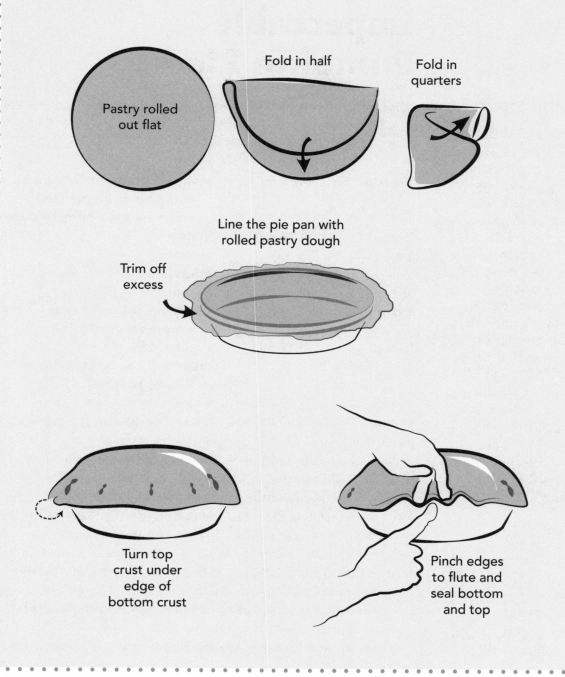

Pastry rolled out flat

Fold in half

Fold in quarters

Line the pie pan with rolled pastry dough

Trim off excess

Turn top crust under edge of bottom crust

Pinch edges to flute and seal bottom and top

Impeccable Pumpkin Pie

Bonus Snack

When you cut open your pumpkin, remove as much of the stringy pulpy goo from the pumpkin seeds as possible (close your eyes and pretend it's a human brain) and place the seeds in a strainer. Rinse under running water and dump them out onto a lightly greased baking sheet. Sprinkle with salt (if you want) and bake at 300°F (150°C) for 30 to 45 minutes, stirring once in a while. They should be golden brown and crisp.

Eat them on a stormy fall night while watching a scary movie on TV.

Guaranteed to be the best pumpkin pie you have ever tasted. No offense to Aunt Betty.

2		eggs
1¾ cups	(425 ml)	pumpkin puree (plain canned pumpkin or homemade puree — see opposite page)
¾ cup	(175 ml)	honey
1 tsp.	(5 ml)	cinnamon
½ tsp.	(2 ml)	ginger
½ tsp.	(2 ml)	nutmeg
1 cup	(250 ml)	whipping cream or canned evaporated milk
½ cup	(125 ml)	regular milk
1		unbaked 9 or 10-inch (23 or 25 cm) pie shell

Preheat the oven to 425°F (220°C). Have the unbaked pie shell ready in a baking pan.

Place all the filling ingredients into the container of a blender and blend until smooth. Gosh, that was hard, wasn't it? Pour filling into the pie shell. (If you are using a 9-inch/23 cm pie shell, you may have just a bit more filling than will fit into the crust. Use the extra to fill a few tart shells, or bake in a custard cup as a bonus dessert.)

Bake the pie for 15 minutes at 425°F (220°C), then reduce the temperature to 350°F (180°C) and continue baking for another 45 minutes, or until a knife slipped into the center of the pie comes out clean. Let cool to room temperature before serving with plenty of whipped cream.

Makes one 9 or 10-inch (23 or 25 cm) pie, 6 to 10 servings.

Start with an actual pumpkin? You've got to be kidding.

No, really! Here's what you do.

First, you'll need the right kind of pumpkin. You want a small one, about 6 to 8 inches (15 to 20 cm) in diameter — sometimes called a pie or sugar pumpkin. Those great big Halloween whoppers are too stringy and watery for baking. Besides, you left yours out on the porch to rot, didn't you?

Now remove the stem and cut the pumpkin in half, top to bottom. Scoop out the seeds and place the pumpkin halves, cut-side-down, on a baking pan. Pour just enough water into the pan to barely cover the bottom. Bake at 400°F (200°C) for 30 minutes, or until a little squishy when you touch the top. Turn the halves over and continue baking for another 10 to 15 minutes to dry out the pumpkin flesh a bit.

Remove from the oven, drain off any juice that may have collected in the pumpkin and let cool for a few minutes. Scoop the pulp out with a spoon, place in a blender or food processor and blend until smooth. If the flesh seems a bit too watery, drain it in a fine strainer set over a bowl to remove the excess liquid. The puree should have the consistency of soft mashed potato. That's all there is to it.

One 6 to 8-inch (15 or 20 cm) pumpkin should give you about 4 cups (1 liter) of pumpkin puree, or enough for two pies and maybe a little extra (for pumpkin bread or something). If you're not going to use it within a day or two, freeze the pulp in recipe-size amounts.

Chocolate Chip Cookie Pie

Imagine your favorite cookie. Now imagine it as a pie. This is it.

2		eggs
½ cup	(125 ml)	all-purpose flour
½ cup	(125 ml)	granulated sugar
½ cup	(125 ml)	brown sugar
1 cup	(250 ml)	butter, melted and cooled slightly
1 cup	(250 ml)	chopped walnuts
1 cup	(250 ml)	semisweet chocolate chips
1		unbaked 8 or 9-inch (20 or 23 cm) piecrust

Preheat the oven to 325°F (160°C). Have the unbaked pie shell ready in a baking pan.

In a large bowl, beat the eggs with an electric mixer or a whisk until foamy. Add the flour, the granulated sugar and the brown sugar, and beat until blended. Stir in the melted butter and the walnuts. Pour into the prepared piecrust and sprinkle the chocolate chips all over the top. The chocolate chips will sink into the filling — possibly all the way to the bottom. That's okay. Bake for 55 to 60 minutes, or until filling is puffed and golden but not dry.

Serve warm with ice cream or whipped cream. And, if you really can't leave well enough alone, perhaps just a drizzle of chocolate sauce.

Makes one 8 or 9-inch (20 or 23 cm) pie, 6 to 8 servings.

Gluten-Free Friendly
Substitute gluten-free flour for the regular all-purpose flour in the filling for this pie. Bake it in a ready-made gluten-free crust.

Fancy French Lemon Tart

Incredibly easy, very lemony and terribly French. Bon appétit!

1 cup	**(250 ml)**	**granulated sugar**
½ cup	**(125 ml)**	**lemon juice (about 2 large lemons)**
4		**eggs**
½ cup	**(125 ml)**	**whipping cream**
1		**8 or 9-inch (20 or 23 cm) unbaked pie shell**
		icing sugar for dusting the top

Preheat the oven to 375°F (190°C). Have the unbaked pie shell ready in a baking pan. For extra French authenticity, you can use an actual tart pan (the kind with shallow sides and a removable bottom), if you happen to have one.

In a mixing bowl, beat together the sugar, lemon juice and eggs with an electric mixer for about 1 minute. Add the cream and beat until combined. Pour into tart shell. Bake for 30 to 40 minutes, or until filling is just set in the middle when you jiggle the pan — it will still be a bit wet. Remove from oven and let cool completely on a rack. Dust the top heavily with icing sugar just before serving. Whipped cream is highly recommended. Also a few fresh berries.

Makes one 8 or 9-inch (20 or 23 cm) tart, 6 to 8 servings.

Oldfangled Vanilla Cream Pie

You've probably forgotten how good a real cream pie can be, so consider this a reminder. Delightfully retro, deliciously creamy and easy as, well, pie. See below for variations on the basic recipe.

Vanilla custard

2 cups	(500 ml)	milk
3		eggs
⅔ cup	(150 ml)	granulated sugar
3 tbsp.	(45 ml)	cornstarch
2 tbsp.	(30 ml)	all-purpose flour
2 tbsp.	(30 ml)	butter
1 tsp.	(5 ml)	vanilla extract

To finish the pie

1 cup	(250 ml)	whipping cream
2 tbsp.	(30 ml)	sugar
1		8 or 9-inch (20 or 23 cm) prepared and fully baked pie shell, either pastry (page 179) or crumb (page 181). See how to bake an empty pie shell on page 195.

First, prepare the vanilla custard filling. In a medium-size saucepan, whisk together the milk, eggs, granulated sugar, cornstarch and flour. Place over medium heat and cook, whisking almost constantly, until the mixture becomes thick and smooth — 5 to 8 minutes. (Don't leave this alone for a second while it's cooking — it will thicken suddenly and without warning.) Remove from heat, stir in the butter and vanilla, and whisk until smooth. Transfer custard to a bowl and place a layer of plastic wrap directly on the surface to keep it from forming a yucky skin. Refrigerate for 1 to 2 hours, until completely cold.

Now you're ready to assemble your fabulous pie. In a bowl, beat the whipping cream with the 2 tbsp. (30 ml) of sugar until the cream forms soft peaks. Peel the plastic wrap off the custard and beat it very briefly so that it's smooth. Gently fold half of the whipped cream into the custard and mix just until combined. Transfer to the prepared pie shell and smooth the top with a spatula. Spread the remaining whipped cream over the top of the custard. Decorate the pie in a suitably tasteful manner — fruit, sprinkles, shaved chocolate, plastic dinosaurs, whatever.

Refrigerate pie for at least 1 hour before serving to allow the custard to set. The filling will firm up slightly as it cools, but will remain pretty soft — so be prepared for somewhat messy slices.

Makes one 8 or 9-inch (20 or 23 cm) pie, 6 to 8 servings.

Variations on a Cream Pie

Banana Cream Pie
Arrange a layer of perfectly ripe banana slices (about 2 bananas' worth) on the bottom of the baked piecrust before pouring in the vanilla custard filling. Decorate the top with additional banana slices.

Chocolate Cream Pie
When you're making the basic vanilla custard, add ½ cup (125 ml) semisweet chocolate chips to the milk mixture in the saucepan. Otherwise, prepare the custard as usual. (For a more intense chocolate flavor, also add 1 square (1 oz./28 g) unsweetened baking chocolate in addition to the chocolate chips.) Decorate the top of the pie with chocolate curls (page 170).

Coconut Cream Pie
Use 1 cup (250 ml) each canned coconut milk and regular milk when preparing the custard, and add 1 cup (250 ml) unsweetened shredded coconut. Decorate the top of the pie with lightly toasted shredded coconut.

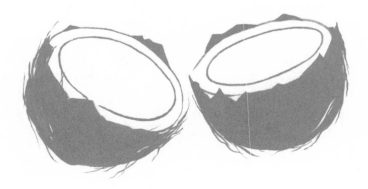

Key Lime Pie

A key lime is a small, yellow-skinned lime with an especially tart flavor, but — unfortunately — they're not always easy to find in stores. We'll just go right ahead and make our key lime pie with plain old green limes and it will be absolutely delicious. So there.

2		eggs
1½ cups	(375 ml)	canned sweetened condensed milk
½ cup	(125 ml)	fresh lime juice
1		8 or 9-inch (20 or 23 cm) graham cracker crust (make it or buy it)
1 cup	(250 ml)	whipping cream
2 tbsp.	(30 ml)	granulated sugar

Preheat the oven to 350°F (180°C). Prebake the graham cracker crust according to directions on page 181.

In a large bowl, beat the eggs with an electric mixer just until foamy. Add the condensed milk, then the lime juice (gradually), and continue beating. The mixture will thicken slightly. Pour into the prepared graham cracker crust. Bake for 10 to 15 minutes — just until set (it should not brown at all). Remove from oven and let cool completely.

Beat the whipping cream with the sugar until stiff and spread over lime filling. Refrigerate pie for at least 1 hour (or up to 1 day) before serving.

Makes one 8 or 9-inch (20 or 23 cm) pie, 6 to 8 servings.

How to bake an empty pie shell

You'd think it would be easy to bake an empty pie shell, wouldn't you? Just roll out the dough, lay it in a pie pan, slam it into the oven — and bingo! A pie shell!

If only this were true.

A pastry shell, alas, does not like to be empty. Without a filling to make it behave, it gets all shrinky in the oven; the pastry slides down the sides of the pan, where it sulks and bloats and becomes quite useless. The only way to get around this is to trick the pastry into thinking it has a filling. This is also known as blind baking. Here's what you do.

Preheat the oven to 425°F (220°C).

Roll out the pastry and place it in a pie plate, as if you were planning to fill it. Cut a piece of foil wrap, waxed paper or parchment paper approximately the size of the pie pan and carefully lay it in the pie shell, covering the pastry. Act casual. Now fill the foil or paper-lined shell with about 4 cups (1 liter) of dry beans (chickpeas are good, but anything will work) to weigh it down. Spread the beans out evenly on the pastry crust.

Place bean-filled crust in the oven and bake for 10 minutes. This will partially set the crust. Now take the pan out of the oven and remove the beans along with the paper or foil lining. Prick the bottom of the pastry all over with a fork. Return the pastry to the oven and bake for another 5 minutes, or until crisp and light golden. Cool and fill. Ha! Piecrust outsmarted again.

Put the beans away and use them again and again, any time you want to blind-bake a pie shell. Just make sure you label them so that you don't accidentally use them in your soup.

The Art
of the Tart

You don't need to buy a special pan to make butter tarts or any other small tarts, for that matter. You can bake perfectly respectable tarts in a muffin pan — something you probably already own. Here's how.

Prepare and roll out your pastry dough a little thinner than you would for a whole pie. Using a large — 3½ to 4-inch (9 to 10 cm) — round cutter, cut out as many circles as possible, reforming the scraps and rerolling until you've used up all the dough. If you don't have an "official" cutter that large, look for anything round to cut the circles: an empty can, a wide glass, a jar lid. One lump of pastry dough (enough for a single piecrust) should make 12 to 14 tart shells.

Carefully press each circle of dough into the compartments of a muffin pan, pleating the sides so that you form a neat shell, with the sides all about the same depth. A little variation is okay, but you don't want your filling spilling over the edges of the pastry. Fill and bake as in the recipe.

Extreme Butter Tarts

Just firm enough not to drip all over your shirt when you bite into one, but runny enough to be utterly delectable. A timeless classic with no redeeming nutritional qualities whatsoever.

1½ cups	(375 ml)	brown sugar
½ cup	(125 ml)	butter, melted
2		eggs
1 tbsp.	(15 ml)	lemon juice
1 tsp.	(5 ml)	vanilla extract
½ cup	(125 ml)	raisins or chopped walnuts (optional — it's a personal thing)
24		unbaked tart shells made with either Foolproof Plain Pastry (page 178) or Flaky Sour Cream Pastry (page 180)

Preheat the oven to 375°F (190°C). Have ready 24 prepared tart shells (see sidebar).

In a mixing bowl, with an electric mixer, beat together the brown sugar, butter, eggs, lemon juice and vanilla until creamy and thick — about 2 or 3 minutes.

If you want raisins or nuts in your butter tarts — purists may object, but you can't please everyone — sprinkle about 1 tsp. (5 ml) into the bottom of each unbaked tart shell. Pour the filling mixture in, dividing it evenly among the tart shells. (If you prefer your butter tarts plain, just omit the raisin/nuts altogether.) Bake for 18 to 20 minutes, until the filling is puffed and golden and the pastry is crisp and very lightly browned.

Makes 24 tarts — enough to share. No, really — you have to.

Spectacular Fresh Fruit Tart

Piled high with a mixture of fresh berries and fruit, this is a showstopper that looks like you spent all day making it. But you didn't.

Easy shortbread crust

1 cup	(250 ml)	all-purpose flour
⅓ cup	(75 ml)	icing sugar
½ cup	(125 ml)	butter

Filling and topping

½ cup	(125 ml)	cream cheese
½ cup	(125 ml)	whipping cream
2 tbsp.	(30 ml)	granulated sugar
½ tsp.	(2 ml)	vanilla extract
3 cups	(750 ml)	mixed fruit or berries (see sidebar)

Have ready a 9-inch (23 cm) tart pan (the kind with removable sides) or a 9-inch (23 cm) pie pan. Either one will work, but the tart pan looks prettier.

First, make the shortbread crust. Combine the flour, icing sugar and butter in the bowl of a food processor. Process, using on-off pulses until the mixture begins to go clumpy and forms a dough. Dump into the tart pan or pie pan and, using your fingers, press the dough firmly and evenly over the bottom and up the sides of the pan. Use a fork to stab some holes into the bottom of the crust and place in the refrigerator to chill for about 30 minutes.

Preheat the oven to 425°F (220°C).

Place the prepared crust in the oven and bake for 13 to 15 minutes — until the crust is lightly browned. Let cool completely.

Now the filling. In a bowl, beat together the cream cheese, whipping cream, sugar and vanilla until smooth and creamy. Spread evenly into the bottom of the cooled crust. Heap all the lovely fruit and berries on top of the cream filling. Serve immediately or refrigerate until ready to serve.

Spectacular.

Makes one 9-inch (23 cm) tart, 6 to 8 servings.

Fruit Tart Toppings

Fruit should be perfectly ripe, peeled, pitted, cored and cut into chunks. Berries should be stemmed and rinsed.

- ✓ Raspberries
- ✓ Strawberries, whole or halved
- ✓ Blackberries
- ✓ Blueberries
- ✓ Kiwi fruit
- ✓ Bananas
- ✓ Pineapple
- ✓ Anything else that's ripe, beautiful and in season

Hot Fudge Brownie Pie

More brownie, really, than pie, but still — it's a fantastic last-minute dessert that should take you no more than ten minutes to make. And about the same amount of time to devour.

3 squares		(1 oz./28 g each) unsweetened chocolate
½ cup	(125 ml)	butter
1¼ cups	(300 ml)	granulated sugar
¼ cup	(60 ml)	all-purpose flour
½ tsp.	(2 ml)	vanilla extract
3		eggs

Preheat the oven to 350°F (180°C). Grease an 8 or 9-inch (20 or 23 cm) pie pan.

In a medium saucepan, melt the chocolate with the butter over very low heat, stirring constantly until smooth. Remove from heat and whisk in the sugar, flour and vanilla, and mix until blended. Add the eggs, one at a time, and whisk until smooth. Pour the batter into the prepared pie pan and bake for 25 to 30 minutes, until just set in the middle, but not dry. The center should remain a little moist — it will firm up as it cools.

Definitely serve warm with ice cream and, oh, go ahead, a drizzle of chocolate sauce.

Makes one 8 or 9-inch (20 or 23 cm) pie, 6 to 8 servings. Or less.

Gluten-Free Friendly
Substitute gluten-free all-purpose flour for the regular all-purpose flour in this recipe. Results may differ slightly from the original version.

Phyllo pastry — a beginner's guide

Poor phyllo. Unfairly feared for its finicky reputation, it is actually a remarkably easy pastry to use. So easy, in fact, that it's practically cheating. After all, you don't even have to make it yourself. So be brave — buy a package and make something. But don't be too smug. After all, there's really nothing to it.

Phyllo pastry is generally available as a frozen product. A 1 lb. (454 g) package contains 18 to 20 paper-thin sheets of pastry, rolled up and tightly wrapped in plastic to prevent the pastry from drying out. To use it, you must defrost the package and handle the sheets of phyllo gently to keep them from tearing or crumbling.

Remove the package of frozen phyllo pastry from the freezer at least 12 hours (or more) before you want to use it and place it in the refrigerator to defrost. Don't try to defrost it at room temperature or in a microwave. Just don't. When you are ready to bake your masterpiece, open the box and remove the sleeve containing the pastry. Unwrap it carefully, then unroll the pastry leaves onto a sheet of waxed paper on a flat surface. Cover the stack of phyllo with a sheet of waxed paper and a dish towel to keep the phyllo from drying out. Follow your recipe and work quickly, using one sheet at a time; keep the remaining pastry covered when it's not being used.

When you are finished making whatever you are making, carefully reroll any remaining pastry, slide it back into the plastic sleeve, seal it tightly and return it to the freezer (or keep it in the refrigerator for up to 2 weeks). Phyllo pastry can safely be refrozen.

Phyllo Tart Shells

Fill these impossibly delicate tart shells with Lemon Curd Filling (page 172), Chocolate Cream Pie filling (page 193) or even just whipped cream and fresh fruit, for a stunning, drop-dead dessert. Without actually dropping dead.

Preheat the oven to 350°F (180°C).

For each tart shell, you will need ½ sheet of phyllo pastry, thawed. (If you are making 12 shells, remove 6 sheets of phyllo pastry from the package, then reroll the remaining phyllo and return it to the freezer. Yes, it's okay to do that.)

Stack the phyllo sheets on a cutting board and, with a sharp knife, cut the rectangular sheets into 6 squarish pieces — cut in half lengthwise and into thirds crosswise. Stack them and work quickly.

Melt ¼ cup (60 ml) butter. Brush the cups of a 12-cup muffin pan very lightly with the butter.

Now take 1 square of phyllo and place it in front of you. Very lightly brush it with a little butter. Place a second sheet of phyllo on top of the first — somewhat on an angle so the corners don't meet— and brush this one lightly with butter too. Finally, place a third square on top, again on an angle — and brush it lightly with butter. Gently press the phyllo into one compartment of the prepared muffin pan so the bottom is flat and the overhanging phyllo is sticking up around the edges. You'll know what I mean when you do it.

Repeat with the remaining phyllo squares. You may find it easier to leave every other compartment of the muffin pan empty because of the overhanging phyllo — you can either use two muffin pans or bake the shells in two batches. Or you can trim off the excess phyllo — but what fun is that?

Bake for 8 to 10 minutes, just until the phyllo is lightly browned around the edges and the shells are crisp. Let cool before filling with something wonderful.

Try to be modest about it, please.

Baklava

The classic Greek pastry. Intensely sweet, very sticky, way too rich and much too buttery. In other words, absolutely perfect in every way.

4 cups	(1 liter)	finely chopped walnuts
½ cup	(125 ml)	granulated sugar
1 tsp.	(5 ml)	cinnamon
1 lb.	(454 g)	phyllo pastry leaves
		(1 package), thawed
¾ cup	(175 ml)	butter, melted
1½ cups	(375 ml)	honey
1 tbsp.	(15 ml)	lemon juice

Preheat the oven to 325°F (160°C). Brush a 9 x 13-inch (23 x 33 cm) rectangular baking pan with some of the melted butter.

In a large bowl, toss together the walnuts, sugar and cinnamon. Set aside.

Unroll the package of phyllo pastry onto a sheet of waxed paper. Cover with a second sheet of waxed paper and a clean dish towel. (The waxed paper will keep the phyllo from drying out and the towel will keep the whole thing weighted down and covered.)

Remove 1 full sheet of phyllo pastry from the stack and place in the baking dish, allowing it to extend up all the sides of the dish to form a sort of shell. Brush lightly with melted butter. Repeat layering the phyllo until you have 6 sheets of phyllo pastry in the baking dish, each brushed with melted butter. Sprinkle with 1 cup (250 ml) of the walnut mixture.

Cut the remaining phyllo pastry sheets crosswise in half. (A half-sheet of phyllo should fit inside the baking dish almost exactly.) Place one of these half-sheets over the walnuts in the baking dish. Brush lightly with butter. Repeat until you have 6 layers of phyllo, each brushed with butter. Sprinkle with 1 cup (250 ml) of the walnut mixture.

Okay, so far we've used half of the walnut mixture.

Continue — 6 sheets of phyllo, 1 cup (250 ml) walnuts, 6 more layers of phyllo, another cup of walnuts and so forth — until all the walnuts are gone. The top layer should be 6 sheets of phyllo pastry (or however many sheets you have left).

Trim away the excess phyllo pastry that's sticking up around the edges of the baking pan (from the bottom layer where you used full sheets to line the pan). Brush the top of the baklava with the remaining melted butter. With a very sharp knife, cut through the top few layers of pastry in a diamond pattern (4 long rows, then diagonally across) and bake for 1 to 1¼ hours, or until the top is golden and crisp.

Just before the baklava is finished baking, combine the honey and the lemon juice in a small saucepan over medium heat, and heat until hot but not boiling. Spoon the hot honey evenly over the baklava as soon as it comes out of the oven. Let baklava cool completely before cutting into diamonds (along the precut lines).

Makes about 24 servings.

Homemade Strudel

There is nothing like a slice of homemade strudel. Unless it's another slice of homemade strudel. Here are two very easy ways to make the most delicious strudel you've ever eaten. A pastry crust will give you a thicker, slightly softer strudel, and phyllo pastry will give you a very crisp, flaky crust. Try both to see which you like best. There is no wrong strudel.

Pastry Crust Strudel

½ recipe (one lump)		Flaky Sour Cream Pastry (page 180)
1 recipe		filling (see options on page 204)
1 tbsp.	(15 ml)	fine, dry bread crumbs

Preheat the oven to 375°F (190°C). Line a cookie sheet with parchment paper.

Dust your table or other work surface lightly with flour. Lightly flour the prepared pastry dough and roll it out with a rolling pin to form a rectangle, approximately 9 x 15 inches (23 x 38 cm). It will be quite thin. That's fine — it's supposed to be thin. Sprinkle the surface evenly with the bread crumbs. Place the dough so that it's crosswise, with the long side closest to you.

Spoon the filling mixture in a thick row, 2 inches (5 cm) thick, about 1 inch (2 cm) in from the edge of the dough nearest you and from the two sides. (Clear as mud? See diagram on page 205.) Now fold the edge of the dough closest to you up over the filling, then fold in the two sides. Carefully roll the strudel away from you, gently but firmly, without tearing the pastry. Lift it carefully and transfer to one of the prepared cookie sheets, seam-side-down. Cut 4 or 5 steam vents into the top of the pastry to allow the filling to breathe.

Bake for 35 to 40 minutes, until the pastry is golden brown and the filling is tender (poke a toothpick through one of the steam vents to check). Let cool before attempting to remove from the pan.

Makes 1 strudel roll, 6 to 8 servings.

Phyllo Crust Strudel

3 sheets		phyllo pastry
2 tbsp.	(30 ml)	butter, melted
2 tbsp.	(30 ml)	fine, dry bread crumbs
1 recipe		filling (see options on page 204)

Preheat the oven to 375°F (190°C). Line a cookie sheet with parchment paper.

Unwrap the phyllo pastry, unroll it and remove 3 sheets from the package. Reroll the remaining phyllo and return it to the package to prevent it from drying out. Lay a clean dish towel on the table or other flat surface. Place 1 sheet of phyllo on the dish towel, brush the phyllo lightly with melted butter and sprinkle evenly with half of the bread crumbs. Place a second sheet of phyllo over the first, brush it with butter and sprinkle with the remaining bread crumbs. Place the third sheet of phyllo on top and brush it with butter. Turn the phyllo so that it's lying crosswise, with a long side closest to you.

Spoon the filling mixture onto the dough in a thick row, 2 inches (5 cm) thick, about 1 inch (2 cm) in from the edge of the dough nearest you and from the two sides. Now fold the bottom edge (the side nearest you) of the dough up over the filling to cover it, and fold in the two sides. Carefully roll the pastry away from you, using the dish towel to help you roll the strudel without tearing the phyllo. Lift it up as gently as possible and place on the prepared cookie sheet, seam-side-down. Brush lightly with the remaining melted butter. Cut a few steam vents into the top of the strudel.

Bake for 35 to 40 minutes, until the pastry is golden brown and the filling is tender. Let cool for at least 15 minutes before attempting to remove from the pan.

Makes 1 strudel roll.

So Many Strudels, So Little Time

Each of the filling mixtures below will fill one strudel roll.

Apple Strudel Filling

3		medium apples
¼ cup	(60 ml)	granulated sugar
1 tbsp.	(15 ml)	all-purpose flour
½ tsp.	(2 ml)	cinnamon
2 tbsp.	(30 ml)	chopped walnuts (optional)
2 tbsp.	(30 ml)	raisins (optional)

Peel, core and thinly slice the apples. You should have 2 cups (500 ml) sliced apples. Mix with sugar, flour and cinnamon — and the nuts and raisins, if you're using them. Toss to coat the apple slices evenly.

Peach Strudel Filling

3		medium peaches
¼ cup	(60 ml)	granulated sugar
1 tbsp.	(15 ml)	all-purpose flour
1 tbsp.	(15 ml)	cornstarch

Peel, pit and thinly slice the peaches. You should have 2 cups (500 ml) peach slices. Mix with sugar, flour and cornstarch. Toss to coat the peach slices evenly.

Blueberry Strudel Filling

2 cups	(500 ml)	fresh (or frozen) blueberries
¼ cup	(60 ml)	granulated sugar
1 tbsp.	(15 ml)	all-purpose flour
1 tbsp.	(15 ml)	cornstarch
1 tsp.	(5 ml)	grated lemon zest

Mix the blueberries with the sugar, flour, cornstarch and lemon zest. If you're using frozen blueberries, don't thaw them. Toss to coat the berries evenly.

Strawberry-Rhubarb Strudel Filling

1 cup	(250 ml)	chopped fresh (or frozen) rhubarb
1 cup	(250 ml)	sliced fresh (or frozen) strawberries
⅓ cup	(75 ml)	granulated sugar
1 tbsp.	(15 ml)	all-purpose flour
1 tbsp.	(15 ml)	cornstarch

Mix the rhubarb and strawberries with the sugar, flour, and cornstarch. Toss to coat the fruit evenly.

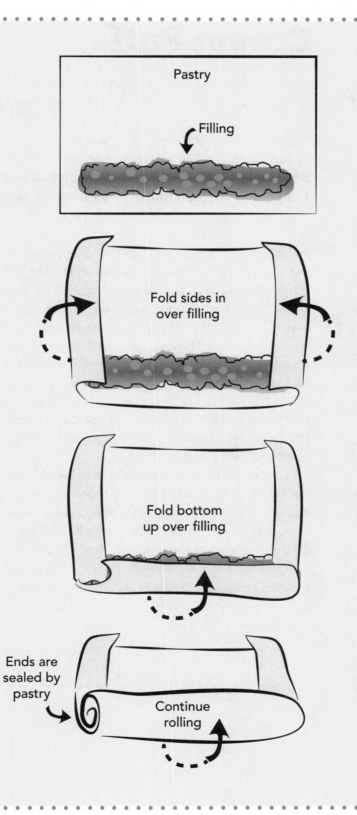

Pastry

Filling

Fold sides in over filling

Fold bottom up over filling

Ends are sealed by pastry

Continue rolling

Cream Puffs

Now what do I do? Cream puff ideas:

✓ Fill with plain or chocolate whipped cream (see page 155) and dust with icing sugar or drizzle with Chocolate Ganache Glaze (see page 171).

✓ Fill with ice cream and top with chocolate sauce.

✓ Fill with vanilla or chocolate custard (see cream pies on page 192) and drizzle with Chocolate Ganache Glaze (see page 171).

✓ Fill with sweetened sliced strawberries mixed with whipped cream (see page 155). Dust with icing sugar.

Astonish your friends and family with a batch of homemade cream puffs. Let them think you are brilliant. Never let on how easy they are to make.

1 cup	**(250 ml)**	**water**
½ cup	**(125 ml)**	**butter**
2 tsp.	**(10 ml)**	**granulated sugar**
1 cup	**(250 ml)**	**all-purpose flour**
4		**eggs**

Preheat the oven to 400°F (200°C). Line one large or two regular-size cookie sheets with parchment paper and grease the paper.

In a medium saucepan, combine water, butter and sugar, and bring to a boil over medium-high heat. Add the flour all at once, reduce the heat to low and cook, stirring constantly, until the mixture leaves the side of the pan and forms a ball. Don't worry — you'll understand what this means when it happens. Remove pan from heat and let cool for a minute or two.

Add the eggs to the flour mixture, 1 at a time, beating with an electric mixer after each egg, until the batter is smooth and glossy. The batter has a tendency to climb up the beaters — just scrape it down and keep going.

Drop the cream puff mixture by heaping spoonfuls (about ¼ cup/60 ml each) onto the prepared cookie sheets. Leave at least 2 inches (5 cm) between the blobs of dough for expansion. They'll puff to more than double their size as they bake. Bake for 35 minutes, then open the oven door and quickly stab a hole into the side of each puff to allow steam inside to escape, then continue to bake for another 5 minutes. The puffs should be crisp and golden brown. Let cool completely, then slice the lid off and fill (see sidebar for ideas).

Makes 12 cream puffs.

Pavlova

A fabulous dessert. Much easier to make than you might imagine. This can be filled with whatever fruits and berries are available. And it's gluten-free!

Meringue shell

3		egg whites, at room temperature
¼ tsp.	(1 ml)	cream of tartar
¾ cup	(175 ml)	granulated sugar, divided
2 tsp.	(10 ml)	cornstarch
1 tsp.	(5 ml)	white vinegar
½ tsp.	(2 ml)	vanilla extract

Pavlova filling

1 cup	(250 ml)	whipping cream
2 tbsp.	(30 ml)	granulated sugar
3 cups	(750 ml)	prepared fruit (see sidebar)

Preheat the oven to 250°F (120°C). Line a cookie sheet or pizza pan with parchment paper and grease the paper.

In a large — obsessively clean — bowl, beat the egg whites and the cream of tartar with an electric mixer until they start to form very soft peaks. (Turn the mixer off and lift the beaters out of the bowl — the meringue should be fluffy but still droopy.) Now add half (pay attention — only half!!!) of the sugar, one spoonful at a time, while beating the mixture constantly, until it forms a stiff and glossy meringue. (The mixture should become stiff enough to form a nondroopy point when you lift the beater out of the bowl.)

In a small bowl, stir together the remaining sugar (you do have some sugar left, don't you?) with the cornstarch. Very gently fold this mixture into the meringue using a rubber spatula, being careful not to deflate the foam. Finally, fold in the vinegar and the vanilla.

Plop the meringue out onto the prepared pan and spread it evenly into a 7 or 8-inch (18 or 20 cm) circle. Build the edges up just a bit to form a rim. Bake for 50 minutes, then turn off the oven without opening the door, and let the meringue cool in the oven for 3 hours.

About 1 hour before you want to serve the pavlova, prepare the filling. Beat the cream with the 2 tbsp. (30 ml) of sugar until it forms soft peaks. Spread the whipped cream in the meringue shell and top with whatever fruit you're using. Serve as soon as possible — the meringue will begin to soften as soon as you've filled it.

Makes 6 to 8 servings.

Mini Pavlovas

For extra fiddliness, instead of baking one big pavlova, form the meringue mixture into eight individual shells before baking (make sure you leave room between them on the baking sheet — they puff). Bake and fill as usual. How cute is that?

Pavlova possibilities:

✓ Strawberries — whole, halved or sliced

✓ Raspberries or blueberries — whole

✓ Kiwi fruit — peeled and sliced or cut into wedges

✓ Peaches — peeled and sliced

✓ Bananas — peeled and sliced

✓ Mangoes — peeled and sliced

Warning: avoid making this dessert on a humid day — the meringue will absorb moisture from the air and become softened and sticky. Surely not what you had in mind.

Clueless Troubleshooting: Pies and Pastries

Nice pie, kiddo. Too bad you had to feed it to the dog. Well, he liked it, anyway. Or maybe he didn't. Check behind the shrubbery. Don't give up hope — you learn from experience.

My piecrust is tough and chewy.
- ✓ You overworked the dough (you slave driver!). Pastry dough should be handled as little and as lightly as possible. You'll know for next time.
- ✓ Reduce the amount of flour slightly.

The pastry is really difficult to roll out without cracking.
- ✓ You may have added too much flour to the dough. Reduce the amount of flour by 1 or 2 tbsp. (15 or 30 ml) next time you make it.
- ✓ Maybe the dough was too cold. Let it warm up to room temperature before rolling.
- ✓ You may be able to rescue the dough by kneading it a few times to make it more pliable and, if necessary, adding a few drops (just a few!) of water to moisten it.

The edges of the crust get brown before anything else is baked.
- ✓ This can happen. If you want to avoid it, cover the outside edges of the crust with a strip of foil halfway through the baking time. This will slow down the browning and keep everything an even color.

The fruit filling leaked out of the pie and all over the floor of the oven.
- ✓ You overfilled the crust. Reduce the amount of filling next time to avoid a blowout.
- ✓ If it was a double-crust pie, maybe the edges weren't sealed tightly. Make sure you fold the top crust under the bottom crust, and pinch the two together firmly (see diagram on page 187). You

can also try moistening the edge of the bottom crust lightly with water before placing the top crust over it, to form a better bond.

✓ But it's still a mess. Just to be safe, next time you bake a pie, place it on a cookie sheet or pizza pan in the oven. This won't prevent the leaking, but it will at least keep it contained.

My cream puffs collapsed.

✓ The insides were probably still soft when you took the cream puffs out of the oven. Next time, after they're finished baking, cut a slit in the side of each puff and leave them in the oven (with the oven off) for at least an hour to dry out.

My pavlova shell is weeping!

✓ Little droplets on the meringue may mean that you've overbaked the shell. Reduce baking time slightly.

✓ Liquid leaking out from under the shell may mean that you've underbaked it. Increase baking time slightly.

✓ Meringue will absorb humidity from the air and can cause droplets on the surface or just a general sogginess. Avoid baking a pavlova on a steamy day.

A Baking Glossary

Bake: To cook in an oven. But you knew that.

Batter: A goopy, semiliquid mixture that, when baked (see above) turns into something delicious: cake, muffins, cookies or whatever. You can't hold batter in your hand. Well, you can — but it will be a mess.

Beat: To mix ingredients energetically (like with an electric mixer) in order to incorporate air and make the mixture fluffy and smooth. Also to prove that you are the boss.

Biscuit: In England, this is a cookie. In the U.S., it's a small flaky quick bread. In Canada, well, it could be either.

Bread: Pretty much anything in a loaf shape. Some breads are sweet and cake-like; others are savory and, well, bready.

Brownie: Usually chocolate. Sometimes not. Usually a square. Occasionally not. Sometimes dense and chewy; sometimes light and cakey; always delicious. Even a bad brownie is better than no brownie at all.

Cake: A wonderful thing made with eggs and flour and sugar and butter. Multilayered and slathered with frosting. Flat and glazed with chocolate or dusted with icing sugar. A cake is, quite simply, magic. Ask any five-year-old.

Chocolate: What? You need a definition? Oh please.

Cookie: A tiny perfect cake. Rolled out and cut into shapes or made from batter dropped onto a baking sheet. Any time of day is cookie time.

Cream: To beat together ingredients like butter and sugar (for example) so that they form a soft, creamy mixture.

Crimp: To make a piecrust look all frilly and pretty by pinching the edges with your fingers. Also known, in certain circles, as fluting.

Crust: The part of a pie that little kids leave on their plates after eating out the filling. Or the outsides of a loaf of bread (see above) that little kids also don't eat. Is there a pattern here?

Cut: To mix solid fat (butter or shortening) into flour by cutting it into teensy-weensy pieces with a pastry blender or a couple of knives. An annoying but (alas) unavoidable technique in pastry making.

Dash: Less than a pinch. But just.

Dough: A thick, pliable mixture of ingredients that you can roll out and cut into cookies or squash into a pan to bake into bread. If you can hold it in your hand without making a mess, it's dough.

Dust: In cooking, to sprinkle lightly with a powdery ingredient like icing sugar — a good thing. In housekeeping, the stuff that's all over the knickknacks in the rumpus room — bad.

Flour: A powdery substance made from grain. Most flour is made from wheat, but other types of flour are made from rice, corn, buckwheat, oat, rye, soy (and so on). Flour is the basis of most of our breads and pastries.

Fold: In baking, to blend one ingredient into another carefully and gently by lifting in big strokes from underneath with a wide spatula. This technique is often used when adding something light and fluffy (like beaten egg whites) to a cake batter, in order to avoid deflating the mixture. In laundry, it's what you do with your pillowcases.

Frosting: The special part of any cake that makes it all worthwhile. Smooth and creamy, frosting can make the difference between just a nice cake and a total religious experience. It can also cover the part of the cake that the dog ate. But don't tell anyone.

Glaze: To cover with a thick, shiny coating — like chocolate or sugar glaze. Glazing a cake is a very effective way of covering up any number of horrible accidents. See also frosting.

Gluten: The stretchy protein in wheat and other types of flour that creates the structure of most standard breads and cakes.

Grease: To coat a baking pan with a nonstick substance that will allow the cake you have slaved over to be removed from the pan without breaking. If it doesn't work, see frosting or glaze.

Knead: To pummel dough into submission in order to force it to become smooth and elastic whether it likes it or not. Highly recommended for stress relief.

Leavening: The ingredient in a recipe that makes the dough or batter puff up when it bakes. Yeast, baking powder, baking soda, even eggs can serve as leavening.

Meringue: A mixture of egg whites and sugar, beaten until stiff. It's what holds up an Angel Food Cake or a Flourless Chocolate Cake and keeps them from collapsing. You can also bake it on its own into crisp dessert shells or cookies.

Mix: To stir together with a fork or spoon or, if all else fails, your hand.

Muffin: A small quick bread, usually sweet, that you can easily devour in the car on the way to work or school.

Phyllo: A paper paper-thin pastry dough, usually bought ready-made (whew), that is used to make delicate pastries like strudel or baklava. Much easier to use than to describe.

Pie: A flattish, round pastry, filled with something or other. It may have a pastry crust, or a crumb crust. It might have apples in it, or chocolate cream, or chicken stew. There's no such thing as a bad pie.

Preheat: Go turn on the oven. Right now. Because you are thinking of baking something, aren't you? By the time your cookies are ready to go into the oven, it will be preheated to just the right temperature. Now, wasn't that clever of you?

Shortening: Any solid or liquid fat. Butter, margarine, solid vegetable shortening, lard and oil are the types of shortening most often used in baking.

Sift: To pass flour or some other powdery ingredient through a fine screen to remove any lumps and fluff it up.

Stir: See mix. Same thing, basically. Except you usually do this with a spoon.

Tart: Sometimes a tart is a tiny single-serving filled pastry shell. Sometimes a tart is a large, straight-sided European-style pie. Once in a while, it's that floozy with the short skirts who works down the hall at the insurance company.

Whip: To beat the living daylights out of egg whites or cream, making them foamy and thick. Like when you make meringue or whipped cream.

Whisk: A wire gadget for whisking. Or is it what you do with a whisk? Whatever. It's a lot like whipping.

Index

Note: Recipes marked "GF" are gluten-free. Those marked "GFF" are "gluten-free friendly" — gluten-free ingredients may be substituted for regular flours and other ingredients.